CORE ENGLISH

Your Life
My Life

CORE ENGLISH

Your Life
My Life

Hellen Matthews, Ronald Caie,
Anne Mitchell and Anne Rigg

SERIES EDITOR:
Colin Lamont

HEINEMANN EDUCATIONAL BOOKS

Heinemann Educational Books Ltd
22 Bedford Square, London WC1B 3HH

LONDON   EDINBURGH   MELBOURNE   AUCKLAND
KINGSTON   SINGAPORE   KUALA LUMPUR   NEW DELHI
IBADAN   NAIROBI   JOHANNESBURG   PORTSMOUTH (NH)

Core English
   Your life, my life. – (Core English)
   1. English literature – 20th century
   I. Matthews, Hellen   II. Series
   820.8'00914   PR1148

   ISBN 0–435–10583–3

First published 1986
Reprinted 1987

Typeset by Fakenham Photosetting Ltd,
Fakenham, Norfolk
Printed and bound in Great Britain by
Richard Clay Ltd, Bungay, Suffolk

CONTENTS

1

Grandmother

By the time I knew my grandmother she was dead.
Before that she was where I thought she stood,
Spectacles, slippers, venerable head,
A standard-issue twinkle in her eyes –
Familiar stage-props of grandmotherhood.
It took her death to teach me they were lies.

My sixteen-year-old knowingness was shocked
To hear her family narrate her past
In quiet nostalgic chorus. As they talked
Her body stiffened on the muted fast
Though well washed linen coverlet of her bed.
The kitchen where we sat, a room I knew,
Took on a strangeness with each word they said.
How she was born where wealth was pennies, grew
Into a woman before she was a girl,
From dirt and pain constructed happiness,
Shed youth's dreams in the fierce sweat of a mill,
Married and mothered in her sixteenth year,
Fed children from her own mouth's emptiness
In an attic rats owned half of, liked her beer.
Careless, they scattered pictures: mother, wife,
Strikes lived through, hard concessions bought and sold
In a level-headed bargaining with life,
Told anecdotes in which her strength rang gold,
Her eyes were clear, her wants as plain as salt.
The past became a mint from which they struck
Small change till that room glittered like a vault.
The corpse in the other room became to me
Awesome as Pharaoh now, as if one look
Would show me all that I had failed to see.

The kitchen became museum in my sight,
Sacred as church. These were the very chairs
In which her gnarled dignity grew frail.
Her hard-won pride had kept these brasses bright.
Her tireless errands were etched upon the stairs.
A vase shone in the sun, holy as grail.
I wanted to bring others to this room,
Say it's nothing else than this that people mean,
A place to which humility can come,
A wrested niche where no one else has been
Won from the wastes of broken worlds and worse.
Here we can stay. Stupid and false, of course.
Themselves to the living is all we have to give.

Let this be
To her, for wreath, gift, true apology.

William McIlvanney

2

Poem for my Sister

My little sister likes to try my shoes,
to strut in them,
admire her spindle-thin twelve-year-old legs
in this season's styles.
She says they fit her perfectly,
but wobbles
on their high heels, they're
hard to balance.

I like to watch my little sister
playing hopscotch,
admire the neat hops-and-skips of her,
their quick peck,
never-missing their mark, not
over-stepping the line.
She is competent at peever.

I try to warn my little sister
about unsuitable shoes,
point out my own distorted feet, the callouses,
odd patches of hard skin.
I should not like to see her
in *my* shoes.
I wish she could stay
sure footed,
       sensibly shod.

Liz Lochhead

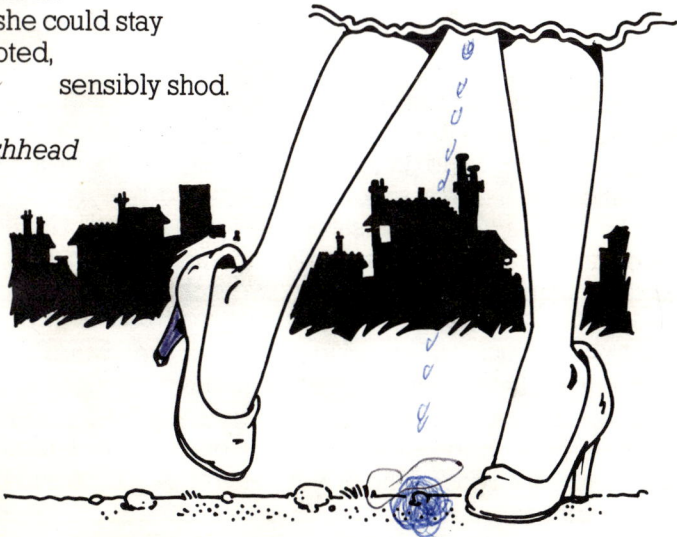

A Child in the Forest

Despite the fact that, unlike Dad, Mam never got her head stuck in a book, she sometimes came up with an original idea that would not have entered his head. Sometimes, she thought it best not to share it with him, as for example, when she had the idea to go scrumping some apples.

On this occasion, I was the lucky one to whom she confided her hopes.

'Bain't stealin', really,' she said, 'you see, they've finished wi' pickin' the apples now for cider an' suchlike, an' them what's left on the ground only goes bad. You an' I could go arter dinner. 'Tis Sunday, so there won't be a lot o' people about. We can take the colander to get a few blackberries from the 'edges of the orchard, in case we do see anybody. We'll pick some elder-berries for your feyther's 'erb tea as well, so everybody'll be satisfied. Mind you, it's a smart step; two miles if it's a yard, an' it's uphill all the road. What d'you say then; d'you want to come with Mam?'

My greedy little stomach would not have owned me had I turned down such an offer. Apples to munch, apples to munch, it made my mouth water to think of them.

'Not 'alf,' I agreed.

With the colander held conspicuously, and two frails rolled unobtrusively under our arms, we started out after dinner, leaving others to wash up and mind the little ones.

We went through the woodland path, the way of us children, as far as the school. Without the busy hum of children's voices, and the comings and goings of little swarms of them in and out of entrances, it had the air of an abandoned beehive.

The hill was now less steep, and was dotted with cottages. 'Nice day', 'warm for the time o' year', and a few incurious stares, and we came to the road where we forked left. Here I was on unfamiliar territory.

''Ere 'tis,' said Mam at long last, as we came to a wide, five-barred gate, with a path leading down through an orchard. Sure enough, speckled among the grass under the trees, were apples; pale green ones and rosy ones, some half-bad, and some nearly all good. There were also apples here and there on the branches.

Beside the gate was a notice – *Trespassers will be Prosecuted.* Even with her glasses on, Mam was very short-sighted, and I was too distracted by the apples to give it a second thought. There was one snag; we were in view of a man working on the land on the opposite side of the road.

Mam outlined our strategy. 'We'll just go in as if we've a right to. Don't pick any apples up yet. There's sure to be some blackberries round the meadows further on. We'll go an' pick some; then when we come back out, we'll fill the frails wi' apples. Wi' bit o' luck thic man will've gone in for 'is tea by then.'

Sure enough, the gate at the other end of this long orchard opened on to a big field that sloped up on the right to a bank with a dip behind it. A few yards down, on the left, some huge blackberry bushes tumbled over the barbed wire fence that separated the meadow from a wild copse of brambles, nettles, and tangled undergrowth.

I had popped about two blackberries in my mouth, and one in the colander, when simultaneously Mam and I became aware of the bull, which had apparently been grazing on the other side of the bank, and was now coming to charge angrily at the intruders.

'Oh, my Gawd, quick! Get over thic wire.' I had never heard Mam sound so alarmed. Without ceremony, or regard for the barbed wire, Mam heaved and pushed me over, then scrambled over herself. By then the bull was practically breathing down her neck.

Shoving, pushing, and pulling me in front of her, she gasped out to keep going; stumbling over a jungle of briars, nettles and other hindrances that clawed at us and stung. It was some yards before I looked up at Mam's face. It was pale ashen grey, lips and all, and beads of sweat had run down, misted up her glasses, and mixed with the blood from the scratches on her face.

'Was we in bad danger, Mam?' I asked.

''Im 'ould 'a killed us, but I reckon thic barbed wire fence 'ave 'alted'n. But be a good little wench and never mind the stings and scratches. The sooner we be out of 'ere the better.' Mam was so breathless it was an effort for her to speak at all.

Unable to see where we were going, we beat down a path with our arms and legs. At last we came to the end of the copse, and to a fence we could climb over on to the edge of a ploughed field. We skirted round this until we came to a gate. Over the gate, and we were on the grass verge of the road again.

'Oh, dear!' said Mam. 'What a sight you be! You do look as though you bin pulled through a 'edge back'ards.' She should have seen herself! We had lost the colander, but miraculously Mam had hung on to the frails. Very dispirited, we started home.

We were soon back by the orchard gate again. The man who had been working opposite was gone.

The apples still lay in the grass. Growing out of the hedge near the gate was an elderflower tree.

'Come on,' said Mam, pulling off a few small branches of the berried elderflower to top the apples with, 'we'll dap in quick while we've got the chance, and fill the frails. Try and pick up the best ones.'

The damp grass had rotted the underside of most of them, but, noses to ground, we darted about under those trees like a pair of well-trained retrievers.

Urged by Mam to be quick, I did not even stop to eat one; anyway I intended, on the way home, to carry some of my load inside my skin. With the frails full to gaping open, we covered the apples with elderberry foliage, and were only yards from safety, when a man coming down the road turned into the gate. Our hearts sank.

With his boots and leggings, battered-brimmed hat above his weather-beaten face, he was obviously a farmer, maybe *the* farmer. Arms akimbo, legs apart, he stood blocking our way, and gruffly asked us what might we be doing in his orchard? His eyes were hard and angry.

So bedraggled were we by this time, he might well have mistaken us for a pair of gypsies.

The shape of the apples bulged out the sides of the straw frails. Red in the face as the rosiest of them, Mam tried to bluff her way out. 'We've just bin gatherin' a few 'erbs for the children's coughs in the winter; we didn't think we was doin' any 'arm.'

'Then you won't mind tipping your bags up for me to see.'

I felt deeply embarrassed, and sorry for Mam; we had escaped a bull, and as far as I could judge, had bumped into a pig. 'It's only a few 'erbs,' Mam lied lamely.

With that he picked up the frails, and tipped the apples out. Then he asked Mam for her name and address; she was near to tears when she told him.

'Pick up your bags, and don't let me catch you on my land again,' he warned us. Mam took her frails, and did not even bother to pick up the elderberries. Downcast and dejected, we carefully closed the orchard gate behind us, under the malevolent eye of the owner.

'The greedy, mingy old fellow!' I exploded, feeling that such a remark was safely above censure in the circumstances, 'all that traipsin' about an' 'ard work for nothin'!'

'Never mind,' said Mam, 'it could 'ave bin wuss. Thic bull might 'ave 'ad us. I only 'ope thic farmer's bark is wuss than 'is bite. I dread to think what'll 'appen if 'im do summons me. After all, 'twouldn't never do for 'im to let people come an' go on 'is land when they pick and choose. If 'im let one do it, 'undreds more 'ould do the same. The pity is that we got caught.'

Under some trees nearer home, Mam stopped, 'Might as well fill up these frails wi' these nice dry bits o' fire 'ood. They do 'elp to boil the kettle real quick for your feyther's cup o' tea on 'is early shift.'

A real mam our Mam was. Perhaps, on second thoughts, that farmer came to the same conclusion, for Mam heard no more from him.

Winifred Foley

4
Baking Day

Thursday was baking day in our house.
The spicy smell of new baked bread would meet
My nostrils when I came home from school and there would be
Fresh buns for tea, but better still were the holidays.

Then I could stay and watch the baking of the bread.
My mother would build up the fire and pull out the damper
Until the flames were flaring under the oven; while it was
     heating
She would get out her earthenware bowl and baking board.

Into the crater of flour in the bowl she would pour sugar
And yeast in hot water; to make sure the yeast was fresh
I had often been sent to fetch it from the grocer that morning,
And it smelt of the earth after rain as it dissolved in the sweet
     water.

Then her small stubby hands would knead and pummel
The dough until they became two clowns in baggy pantaloons,
And the right one, whose three fingers and blue stump
Told of the accident which followed my birth, became whole.

As the hands worked a creamy elastic ball
Took shape and covered by a white cloth was set
On a wooden chair by the fire slowly to rise:
To me the most mysterious rite of all.

From time to time I would peep at the living dough
To make sure it was not creeping out of the bowl.
Sometimes I imagined it possessed, filling the whole room,
And we helpless, unable to control its power to grow,

But as it heaved above the rim of the bowl mother
Was there, taking it and moulding it into plaited loaves
And buns and giving me a bit to make into a bread man,
With currant eyes, and I, too, was a baker.

Rosemary Joseph

5

My Papa's Waltz

The whiskey on your breath
Could make a small boy dizzy;
But I clung on like death:
Such waltzing was not easy.

We romped until the pans
Slid from the kitchen shelf;
My mother's countenance
Could not unfrown itself.

The hand that held my wrist
Was battered on one knuckle;
At every step you missed
My right ear scraped a buckle.

You beat time on my head
With a palm caked hard by dirt,
Then waltzed me off to bed
Still clinging to your shirt.

Theodore Roethke

6

Danny, the Champion of the World

My father put a match to the wick of the lamp hanging from the ceiling and the little yellow flame sprang up and filled the inside of the caravan with pale light. 'How about a hot drink?' he said.

'Yes, please.'

He lit the paraffin burner and put the kettle on to boil.

'I have decided something,' he said. 'I am going to let you in on the deepest darkest secret of my whole life.'

I was sitting up in my bunk watching my father.

'You asked me where I had been,' he said. 'The truth is I was up in Hazell's Wood.'

'Hazell's Wood!' I cried. 'That's miles away!'

'Six miles and a half,' my father said. 'I know I shouldn't have gone and I'm very, very sorry about it, but I had such a powerful yearning ...' His voice trailed away into nothingness.

'But why would you want to go all the way up to Hazell's Wood?' I asked.

He spooned cocoa powder and sugar into two mugs, doing it very slowly and levelling each spoonful as though he were measuring medicine.

'Do you know what is meant by poaching?' he asked.

'Poaching? Not really, no.'

'It means going up into the woods in the dead of night and coming back with something for the pot. Poachers in other places poach all sorts of different things, but around here it's always pheasants.'

'You mean *stealing* them?' I said, aghast.

'We don't look at it that way,' my father said. 'Poaching is an art. A great poacher is a great artist.'

'Is that actually what you were doing in Hazell's Wood, Dad? Poaching pheasants?'

'I was practising the art,' he said. 'The art of poaching.'

I was shocked. My own father a thief! This gentle lovely man! I couldn't believe he would go creeping into the woods at night to pinch valuable birds belonging to somebody else. 'The kettle's boiling,' I said.

'Ah, so it is.' He poured the water into the mugs and brought mine over to me. Then he fetched his own and sat with it at the end of my bunk.

'Your grandad,' he said, 'my own dad, was a magnificent and splendiferous poacher. It was he who taught me all about it. I caught the poaching fever from him when I was ten years old and I've never lost it since. Mind you, in those days just about every man in our village was out in the woods at night poaching pheasants. And they did it not only because they loved the sport but because they needed food for their families. When I was a boy, times were bad for a lot of people in England. There was very little work to be had anywhere, and some families were literally starving. Yet a few miles away in the rich man's wood, thousands of pheasants were being fed like kings twice a day. So can you blame my dad for going out occasionally and coming home with a bird or two for the family to eat?'

'No,' I said. 'Of course not. But we're not starving here, Dad.'

'You've missed the point, Danny boy! You've missed the whole point! Poaching is such a fabulous and exciting sport that once you start doing it, it gets into your blood and you can't give up! Just imagine,' he said, leaping off the bunk and waving his mug in the air, 'just imagine for a minute that you are all alone up there in the dark wood, and the wood is full of keepers hiding behind the trees and the keepers have guns ...'

'Guns!' I gasped. 'They don't have guns!'

'All keepers have guns, Danny. It's for the vermin mostly, the foxes and stoats and weasels who go after the pheasants. But they'll always take a pot at a poacher, too, if they spot him.'

'Dad, you're joking.'

'Not at all. But they only do it from behind. Only when you're trying to escape. They like to pepper you in the legs at about fifty yards.'

'They can't do that!' I cried. 'They could go to prison for shooting someone!'

'You could go to prison for poaching,' my father said. There was a glint and a sparkle in his eyes now that I had never seen before. 'Many's the night when I was a boy, Danny, I've gone into the kitchen and seen my old dad lying face down on the table and Mum standing over him digging the gunshot pellets out of his backside with a potato-knife.'

'It's not true,' I said, starting to laugh.

'You don't believe me?'

'Yes, I believe you.'

'Towards the end, he was so covered in tiny little white scars he looked exactly like it was snowing.'

'I don't know why I'm laughing,' I said. 'It's not funny, it's horrible.'

'"Poacher's bottom" they used to call it,' my father said. 'And there wasn't a man in the whole village who didn't have a bit of it one way or another. But my dad was the champion. How's the cocoa?'

'Fine, thank you.'

'If you're hungry we could have a midnight feast?' he said.

'Could we, Dad?'

'Of course.'

My father got out the bread-tin and the butter and cheese and started making sandwiches.

'Let me tell you about this phony pheasant-shooting business,' he said. 'First of all, it is practised only by the rich. Only the very rich can afford to rear pheasants just for the fun of shooting them down when they grow up. These wealthy idiots spend huge sums of money every year buying baby pheasants from pheasant farms and rearing them in pens until they are big enough to be put out into the woods. In the woods, the young birds hang around like flocks of chickens. They are guarded by keepers and fed twice a day on the best corn until they're so fat they can hardly fly. Then beaters are hired who walk through the woods clapping their hands and making as much noise as they can to drive the half-tame pheasants towards the half-baked men and their guns. After that, it's *bang bang bang* and down they come. Would you like strawberry jam on one of these?'

'Yes, please,' I said. 'One jam and one cheese. But Dad . . .'

'What?'

'How do you actually catch the pheasants when you're poaching? Do you have a gun hidden away up there?'

'A gun!' he cried, disgusted. 'Real poachers don't *shoot* pheasants, Danny, didn't you know that? You've only got to fire a *cap-pistol* up in those woods and the keepers'll be on you.'

'Then how do you do it?'

'Ah,' my father said, and the eyelids drooped over the eyes, veiled and secretive. He spread strawberry jam thickly on a piece of bread, taking his time.

'These things are big secrets,' he said. 'Very big secrets indeed. But I reckon if my father could tell them to me, then maybe I can tell them to you. Would you like me to do that?'

'Yes,' I said. 'Tell me now.'

Roald Dahl

12

7

In Memory of My Grandfather

Swearing about the weather he walked in
like an old tree and sat down;
his beard charred with tobacco, his voice
rough as the bark of his cracked hands.

Whenever he came it was the wrong time.
Roots spread over the hearth, tripped
whoever tried to move about the room;
the house was cramped with only furniture.

But I was glad of his coming. Only
through him could I breathe in the sun
and smell of fields. His clothes reeked
of the soil and the world outside;

geese and cows were the colour he made them,
he knew the language of birds and brought them
singing out of his beard, alive
to my blankets. He was winter and harvest.

Plums shone in his eyes when he rambled
of orchards. With giant thumbs he'd split
an apple through the core, and juice
flowed from his ripe, uncultured mouth.

Then, hearing the room clock chime,
he walked from my ceiling of farmyards
and returned to his forest of thunder;
the house regained silence and corners.

Slumped there in my summerless season
I longed for his rough hands and words
to break the restrictions of my bed,
to burst like a tree from my four walls.

But there was no chance again of miming
his habits or language. Only now,
years later in a cramped city, can I
be grateful for his influence and love.

Edward Storey

8
Luke Baldwin's Vow

That summer when twelve-year-old Luke Baldwin came to live with his Uncle Henry in the house on the stream by the sawmill, he did not forget that he had promised his dying father he would try to learn things from his uncle; so he used to watch him very carefully.

Uncle Henry, who was the owner of the sawmill, was a big, burly man weighing more than sixteen stone, and he had a rough-skinned, brick-coloured face. He looked like a powerful man, but his health was not good. He had aches and pains in his back and shoulders which puzzled the doctor.

The first thing Luke learned about Uncle Henry was that everybody had great respect for him. The four men he employed in the sawmill were always polite and attentive when he spoke to them. His wife, Luke's Aunt Helen, a kindly, plump, straightforward woman, never argued with him. 'You should try and be like your Uncle Henry,' she would say to Luke. 'He's so wonderfully practical. He takes care of everything in a sensible, easy way.'

Luke used to trail round the sawmill after Uncle Henry not only because he liked the fresh clean smell of the newly-cut wood and the big piles of sawdust, but because he was impressed by his uncle's precise, firm tone when he spoke to the men.

Sometimes Uncle Henry would stop and explain to Luke something about a piece of timber. 'Always try to learn the essential facts, son,' he would say. 'If you've got the facts, you know what's useful and what isn't useful, and no one can fool you.'

He showed Luke that nothing of value was ever wasted around the mill. Luke used to listen, and wonder if there were another man in the world who knew so well what was needed and what ought to be thrown away.

Uncle Henry had known at once that Luke needed a bicycle to ride to his school, which was two miles away in town, and he bought him a good one. He knew that Luke needed good, serviceable clothes. He also knew exactly how much Aunt Helen needed to run the house, the price of everything, and how much a woman should be paid for doing the rough housework.

In the evenings Luke used to sit in the sitting-room watching his uncle making notations in a black notebook which he always carried in his vest pocket, and he knew that he was assessing all the transactions of the day.

Luke promised himself that when he grew up he too would be admired for his good, sound judgment. But, of course, he couldn't always be watching and learning from Uncle Henry, for too often when he watched him he thought of his own father: then he was lonely. So he began to build up another secret life for himself at the sawmill, and his companion was the eleven-year-old collie, Dan, a dog blind in one eye and with a slight limp in his left hind leg.

Dan was a fat, slow-moving old dog. He was very affectionate and his eye was the colour of amber. His fur was amber too. When Luke left for school in the morning, the old dog followed him for half a mile down the road, and when he returned in the afternoon there was Dan waiting at the gate.

Sometimes they would play round the millpond or by the dam, or go down the stream to the lake. Luke was never lonely when the dog was with him. There was an old rowing boat they used as a pirate ship in the stream, and they would be pirates together, with Luke shouting instructions to Captain Dan and with the dog seeming to understand and wagging his tail enthusiastically. Its amber eye was alert, intelligent and approving. Then they would plunge into the copse on the other side of the stream, pretending they were hunting tigers. Of course, the old dog was no longer much good for hunting: he was too slow and too lazy. Uncle Henry no longer used him for hunting rabbits or anything else.

When they came out of the copse, they would lie together on the cool, grassy bank being affectionate with each other, with Luke talking earnestly, while the collie, as Luke believed, smiled with the good eye. Lying in the grass, Luke would say things to Dan he could not say to his uncle or aunt. Not that what he said was important; it was just stuff about himself that he might have told to his own father or mother if they had been alive. Then they would go back to the house for lunch, and after lunch Dan would follow him down the road to Mr Kemp's house, where they would ask old Mr Kemp if they could go with him to round up his four cows. The old man was always glad to see them. He seemed to like watching Luke and the collie pretending they were cowboys.

Uncle Henry no longer paid much attention to the collie, though once when he tripped over him on the verandah, he

shook his head and said thoughtfully, 'Poor old fellow, he's through. Can't use him for anything. He just eats and sleeps and gets in the way.'

One Sunday during Luke's summer holidays when they had returned from church and had had their lunch, they all moved out to the verandah where the collie was sleeping. Luke sat down on the step, his back against the verandah post. Uncle Henry took the rocking chair, and Aunt Helen stretched herself out in a deck-chair, sighing contentedly. Then Luke, eyeing the collie, tapped the step with the palm of his hand, giving three little taps like a signal and the old collie, lifting his head, got up stiffly with a slow wagging of the tail as an acknowledgement that the signal had been heard, and began to cross the verandah to Luke.

But the dog was sleepy; his bad eye was turned to the rocking chair; in passing, his left front paw went under the rocker. With a frantic yelp, the dog went bounding down the steps and hobbled round the corner of the house, where he stopped, hearing Luke coming after him. All he needed was the touch of Luke's hand. Then he began to lick the hand methodically, as if apologising.

'Luke,' Uncle Henry called sharply, 'bring that dog here.'

16

When Luke led the collie back to the verandah, Uncle Henry nodded and said, 'Thanks, Luke.' Then he took out a cigarette, lit it, put his big hands on his knees and began to rock in the chair while he frowned and eyed the dog steadily. Obviously he was making some kind of important decision about the collie.

'What's the matter, Uncle Henry?' Luke asked nervously.

'That dog can't see any more,' Uncle Henry said.

'Oh yes, he can,' Luke said quickly. 'His bad eye got turned to the chair, that's all, Uncle Henry.'

'And his teeth are gone, too,' Uncle Henry went on, paying no attention to what Luke had said. Turning to the deck-chair he called, 'Helen, sit up a minute, will you?'

When she got up and stood beside him, he went on, 'I was thinking about this old dog the other day, Helen. It's not only that he's just about blind, but did you notice that when we drove up after church he didn't even bark?'

'It's a fact he didn't, Henry.'

'No, not much good even as a watchdog now.'

'Poor old fellow. It's a pity, isn't it?'

'And no good for hunting. He eats a lot, I suppose.'

'About as much as he ever did, Henry.'

'The plain fact is the old dog isn't worth his keep any more. It's time we got rid of him.'

'It's always so hard to know how to get rid of a dog, Henry.'

'I was thinking about it the other day. Some people think it's best to shoot a dog. I haven't had any cartridges for that shotgun for over a year. Poisoning is a hard death for a dog. Perhaps drowning is the easiest and quickest way. Well, I'll speak to one of the mill hands and get him to look after it.'

Crouching on the ground, his arms round the old collie's neck, Luke cried out, 'Uncle Henry, Dan's a wonderful dog! You don't know how wonderful he is!'

'He's just a very old dog, son,' Uncle Henry said calmly. 'The time comes when you have to get rid of any old dog. We've got to be practical about it. I'll get you a pup, son. A smart little dog that'll be worth its keep. A pup that will grow up with you.'

'I don't want a pup!' Luke cried, turning his face away. Circling round him, the dog began to bark, then flick his long pink tongue at the back of Luke's neck.

Aunt Helen, catching her husband's eye, put her finger on her lips, warning him not to go on talking in front of the boy.

But Luke was frightened, for he knew what his uncle was like. He knew that if his uncle had decided that the dog was useless and that it was sane and sensible to get rid of it, he would be ashamed of himself if he were diverted by any sentimental considerations. Luke knew in his heart that he couldn't move his uncle. All he could do, he thought, was to keep the dog away from his uncle, keep him out of the house, feed him when Uncle Henry wasn't about.

Next day at noon Luke saw his uncle walking from the mill towards the house with old Sam Carter, a mill hand. Sam Carter was a dull, stooped, slow-witted man of sixty with an iron-grey beard. He hardly ever spoke to anybody.

Watching from the verandah, Luke noticed that his uncle suddenly gave Sam Carter a cigarette, which Sam put in his pocket. Luke had never seen his uncle give Sam a cigarette or pay much attention to him.

Then, after lunch, Uncle Henry said lazily that he would like Luke to take his bicycle and go into town and get him some tobacco.

'I'll take Dan,' Luke said.

'Better not, son,' Uncle Henry said. 'It'll take you all afternoon. I want that tobacco. Go along, Luke.

His uncle's tone was so casual that Luke tried to believe they were not merely getting rid of him. Of course he had to do what he was told. He had never dared to refuse to obey an order from his uncle. But when he had taken his bicycle and had ridden down the lane that followed the stream to the main road and had got about a quarter of a mile along the road, he found that all he could think of was his uncle handing old Sam Carter the cigarette.

Slowing down, sick with worry now, he got off the bike and stood uncertainly on the sunlit road. Sam Carter was a gruff, aloof old man who would have no feeling for a dog. Then suddenly Luke could go no farther without getting some assurance that the collie would not be harmed while he was away. Across the fields he could see the house.

Leaving the bike in the ditch, he started to cross the fields, intending to get close enough to the house so Dan could hear him if he whistled softly. He got about fifty yards away from the house and whistled and waited, but there was no sign of the dog.

For a few minutes Luke couldn't make up his mind what to do, then he decided to go back to the road, get on his bike and go back the way he had come until he got to the place where the lane joined the road. There he could leave his bike, go up the lane, then into the tall grass and get close to the front of the house and the sawmill without being seen.

He had followed the drive for about a hundred yards, and

when he came to the place where the river began to bend sharply towards the house his heart fluttered and his legs felt paralysed, for he saw the old boat in the one place where the river was deep, and in the boat was Sam Carter with the collie.

The bearded man in the blue overalls was smoking the cigarette; the dog, with a rope round its neck, sat contentedly beside him, its tongue going out in a friendly lick at the hand holding the rope. It was all like a crazy dream picture to Luke: all wrong because it looked so lazy and friendly, even the curling smoke from Sam Carter's cigarette.

But as Luke cried out, 'Dan, Dan! Come on, boy!' and the dog jumped at the water, he saw that Sam Carter's left hand was hanging deep in the water, holding a foot of rope with a heavy stone at the end. As Luke cried out wildly, 'Don't! Please don't!' Carter dropped the stone, for the cry came too late: it was blurred by the screech of the bit saws at the mill. But Carter was startled, and he stared stupidly at the riverbank, then he ducked his head and began to row quickly to the bank.

But Luke was watching the collie take what looked like a long, shallow dive, except that the hind legs suddenly kicked up above the surface, then shot down, and while he watched, Luke sobbed and trembled, for it was as if the happy secret part of his life round the sawmill was being torn away from him. But even while he watched, he seemed to be following a plan without knowing it, for he was already fumbling in his pocket for his jack-knife, jerking the blade open, kicking his shoes off while he muttered fiercely and prayed that Sam Carter would get out of sight.

It hardly took the mill hand a minute to reach the bank and go slinking furtively round the bend as if he felt the boy was following him. But Luke hadn't taken his eyes off the exact spot in the water where Dan had disappeared. As soon as the mill hand was out of sight, Luke slid down the bank and took a leap at the water, the sun glistening on his slender body, his eyes wild with eagerness as he ran out to the deep place, then arched his back and dived, swimming under water, his open eyes getting used to the greenish-grey haze of the water, the sandy bottom and the imbedded rocks.

His lungs began to ache, then he saw the shadow of the collie floating at the end of the taut rope, rock-held in the sand. He slashed at the rope with his knife. He couldn't get much strength in his arm because of the resistance of the water. He grabbed the rope with his left hand, hacking with his knife. The collie began to drift up slowly, like a water-soaked log. Then his own

head shot above the surface, and while he was sucking in the air he was drawing the rope, pulling the collie towards him and treading water. In a few strokes he was away from the deep place and his feet touched the bottom.

Hoisting the collie out of the water, he scrambled towards the bank, lurching and stumbling in front because the collie felt like a dead weight.

He went on up the bank and across the path to the tall grass, where he fell flat, hugging the dog and trying to warm him with his own body. But the collie didn't stir, the good amber eye remained closed. Then suddenly Luke wanted to act like a resourceful, competent man.

Getting up on his knees, he stretched the dog out on its belly, drew him between his knees, felt with trembling hands for the soft places on the flanks just above the hipbones, and rocked back and forth, pressing with all his weight, then relaxing the pressure as he straightened up. He hoped that he was working the dog's lungs like a bellows. He had read that men who had been thought drowned had been saved in this way.

'Come on, Dan. Come on, old boy,' he pleaded softly. As a little water came from the collie's mouth, Luke's heart jumped, and he muttered over and over, 'You can't be dead, Dan! You can't, you can't! I won't let you die, Dan!' He rocked back and forth tirelessly, applying the pressure to the flanks. More water dribbled from the mouth. In the collie's body he felt a faint tremor. 'Oh gosh, Dan, you're alive,' he whispered. 'Come on, boy. Keep it up.'

With a cough the collie suddenly jerked his head back, the amber eye opened, and there they were looking at each other. Then the collie, thrusting his legs out stiffly, tried to hoist himself up, staggered, tried again, then stood there in a stupor. He shook himself like any other wet dog, turned his head, eyed Luke, and the red tongue came out in a weak flick at Luke's cheek.

'Lie down, Dan,' Luke said. As the dog lay down beside him, Luke closed his eyes, buried his head in the wet fur and wondered why all the muscles of his arms and legs began to jerk in a nervous reaction now that it was all over.

'Stay there, Dan,' he said softly, and went back to the path, got his shoes and came back beside Dan and put them on. 'I think we'd better get away from this spot, Dan,' he said. 'Keep down, boy. Come on.' And he crawled on through the tall grass till they were about seventy-five yards from the house. There they lay down together.

In a little while he heard his aunt's voice calling, 'Luke. Oh, Luke! Come here, Luke!'

'Quiet, Dan,' Luke whispered. A few minutes passed, and then Uncle Henry called, 'Luke, Luke!' and he began to come down the path. They could see him standing there, massive and imposing, his hands on his hips as he looked down the path, then he turned and went back to the house.

As he watched the sunlight shine on the back of his uncle's neck, the exultation Luke had felt at knowing the collie was safe beside him turned to bewildered despair, for he knew that even if he should be forgiven for saving the dog when he saw it drowning, the fact was that his uncle had been thwarted. His mind was made up to get rid of Dan, and in a few days' time, in another way, he would get rid of him, as he got rid of anything at the mill that he believed to be useless or a waste of money.

As he lay back and looked up at the hardly-moving clouds, he began to grow frightened. He couldn't go back to the house, nor could he take the collie into the woods and hide him and feed him there unless he tied him up. If he didn't tie him up, Dan would wander back to the house.

'I suppose there's just nowhere we can go, Dan,' he whispered sadly. 'Even if we start off along the road, somebody will see us.'

But Dan was watching a butterfly that was circling crazily above them. Raising himself a little, Luke looked through the grass at the corner of the house, then he turned and looked the other way to the wide blue lake. With a sigh he lay down again, and for hours they lay there together, until there was no sound from the saws in the mill and the sun moved low in the western sky.

'Well, we can't stay here any longer, Dan,' he said at last. 'We'll just have to get as far away as we can. Keep down, old boy,' and he began to crawl through the grass, going farther away from the house. When he could no longer be seen, he got up and began to run across the field towards the road leading to town.

On the road the collie would turn from time to time as if wondering why Luke shuffled along, dragging his feet wearily, his head down. 'I'm stumped, that's all, Dan,' Luke explained. 'I can't seem to think of a place to take you.'

When they were passing the Kemps' house they saw the old man sitting in the garden, and Luke stopped. All he could think of was that Mr Kemp had liked them both and it had been a pleasure to help him fetch the cows in the evening. Dan had always been with them. Staring at the figure of the old man in the garden, he said in a worried tone, 'I wish I could be sure of him, Dan. I wish he was a dumb, stupid man who wouldn't know or care whether you were worth anything ... Well, come on.' He opened the gate bravely, but he felt shy and unimportant.

'Hello, son. What's on your mind?' Mr Kemp called from the lawn. He was a thin, wiry man in a cream-coloured shirt. He had a grey, untidy moustache, his skin was wrinkled and leathery, but his eyes were always friendly and amused.

'Could I speak to you, Mr Kemp?' Luke asked.

'Of course.'

'It's about Dan. He's a great dog, but I expect you know that as well as I do. I was wondering if you could keep him here for me.'

'Why should I keep Dan here, son?'

'Well, it's like this,' Luke said, fumbling for words awkwardly: 'My uncle won't let me keep him any more ... says he's too old.' His mouth began to tremble, then he blurted out the story.

'I see, I see,' Mr Kemp said slowly, and he got up and began to stroke the collie's head. 'Of course, Dan's an old dog, son,' he said quietly. 'And sooner or later you've got to get rid of an old dog. Your uncle knows that. Perhaps it's true that Dan isn't worth his keep.'

'He doesn't eat much, Mr Kemp. Just one meal a day.'

'I wouldn't want you to think your uncle was cruel and unfeeling, Luke,' Mr Kemp went on. 'He's a fine man ... perhaps just a little bit too practical and straightforward.'

'I suppose that's it,' Luke agreed, but he was really waiting and trusting the expression in the old man's eyes.

'Perhaps you should make him a practical proposition.'

'I – I don't know what you mean.'

'Well, beginning with the way you get the cows for me in the evenings,' Mr Kemp said, smiling to himself. 'In fact, I don't think you need me to go along with you at all. Now, supposing I gave you half a crown a week. Would you get the cows in for me every night?'

'Of course I would, Mr Kemp. I like doing it, anyway.'

'All right, son. It's a deal. Now I'll tell you what to do. Go back to your uncle, and before he has a chance to open up on you, you say right out that you've come to him with a business proposition. Say it like a man, just like that. Offer to pay him the half a crown a week for the dog's keep.'

'But my uncle doesn't need half a crown, Mr Kemp,' Luke said uneasily.

'Of course not,' Mr Kemp agreed. 'It's the principle of the thing. Be confident. Remember that he's got nothing against the dog. Go on, son. Let me know how you do,' he added, with an amused smile. 'If I know your uncle at all, I think it'll work.'

'I'll try it, Mr Kemp,' Luke said. 'Thanks very much.' But he didn't have any confidence, for even though he knew that Mr Kemp was a wise old man who would not deceive him, he couldn't believe that half a crown a week would stop his uncle, who was an important man. 'Come on, Dan,' he called, and he went slowly and apprehensively back to the house.

When they were going up the path, his aunt cried from the open window, 'Henry, Henry, in heaven's name, it's Luke with Dan!'

Ten paces from the verandah, Luke stopped and waited nervously for his uncle to come out. Uncle Henry came out in a rush, but when he saw the collie and Luke standing there, he stopped stiffly, turned pale and his mouth hung open loosely.

'Luke,' he whispered, 'that dog had a stone round his neck.'

'I fished him out of the stream,' Luke said uneasily.

'Oh. Oh, I see,' Uncle Henry said, and gradually the colour came back to his face. 'You fished him out, eh?' he asked, still looking at the dog uneasily. 'Well, you shouldn't have done that. I told Sam Carter to get rid of the dog, you know.'

'Just a minute, Uncle Henry,' Luke said, trying not to falter. He gained confidence as Aunt Helen came out and stood beside her husband, for her eyes seemed to be gentle, and he went on bravely, 'I want to make you a practical proposition, Uncle Henry.'

'A what?' Uncle Henry asked, still feeling insecure, and wishing the boy and the dog weren't confronting him.

'A practical proposition,' Luke blurted out quickly. 'I know Dan isn't worth his keep to you. I don't suppose he's worth anything to anybody but me. So I'll pay you half a crown a week for his keep.'

'What's this?' Uncle Henry asked, looking bewildered. 'Where would you get half a crown a week, Luke?'

'I'm going to get the cows in every night for Mr Kemp.'

'Oh, for heaven's sake, Henry,' Aunt Helen pleaded, looking distressed, 'let him keep the dog!' and she fled into the house.

'None of that kind of talk!' Uncle Henry called after her. 'We've got to be sensible about this!' But he was shaken himself, and overwhelmed with a distress that destroyed all his confidence. As he sat down slowly in the rocking chair and stroked the side of his big face, he wanted to say weakly, 'All right, keep the dog, but he was ashamed of being so weak and sentimental. He stubbornly refused to yield to this emotion; he was trying desperately to turn his emotion into a bit of good useful commonsense, so he could justify his distress. So he rocked and pondered.

At last he smiled. 'You're a smart young fellow, Luke,' he said slowly. 'Imagine you working it out like this. I'm tempted to accept your proposition.'

'Oh, thanks, Uncle Henry.'

'I'm accepting it because I think you'll learn something out of this,' he went on ponderously. 'You'll learn that useless luxuries cost the smartest of men hard-earned money.'

'I don't mind.'

'Well, it's a thing you'll have to learn sometime. I think you'll learn, too, because you certainly seem to have a practical streak in you. It's a streak I like to see in a boy. All right, son,' he said, and he smiled with relief and went into the house.

Turning to Dan, Luke whispered softly, 'Well, what do you know about that?'

As he sat down on the step with the collie beside him and listened to Uncle Henry talking to his wife, he began to glow with exultation. Then gradually his exultation began to change to a vast wonder that Mr Kemp should have had such a perfect understanding of Uncle Henry. He began to dream of someday being as wise as old Mr Kemp and knowing exactly how to handle people. It was possible, too, that he had already learned some of the things about his uncle that his father had wanted him to learn.

Putting his head down on the dog's neck, he vowed to himself fervently that he would always have some money on hand, no matter what became of him, so that he would be able to protect all that was truly valuable from the practical people in the world.

Morley Callaghan

9
The Kitten

The feet were tramping directly towards her. In the hot darkness under the tarpaulin the cat cuffed a kitten to silence and listened intently.

She could hear the scuffling and scratching of hens about the straw-littered yard; the muffled grumbling of the turning churn in the dairy; the faint clink and jangle of harness from the stable – drowsy, comfortable, reassuring noises through which the clang of the iron-shod boots on the cobbles broke ominously.

The boots ground to a halt, and three holes in the cover, brilliant diamond-points of light, went suddenly black. Crouching, the cat waited, then sneezed and drew back as the tarpaulin was thrown up and glaring white sunlight struck at her eyes.

She stood over her kittens, the fur of her back bristling and the pupils of her eyes narrowed to pin-points. A kitten mewed plaintively.

For a moment, the hired man stared stupidly at his discovery, then turned towards the stable and called harshly: 'Hi, Maister! Here a wee.'

A second pair of boots clattered across the yard, and the face of the farmer, elderly, dark and taciturn, turned down on the cats.

'So that's whaur she's been,' commented the newcomer slowly.

He bent down to count the kittens and the cat struck at him, scoring a red furrow across the back of his wrist. He caught her by the neck and flung her roughly aside. Mewing she came back and began to lick her kittens. The Master turned away.

'Get rid of them,' he ordered. 'There's ower many cats aboot this place.'

'Aye, Maister,' said the hired man.

Catching the mother he carried her, struggling and swearing, to the stable, flung her in, and latched the door. From the loft he secured an old potato sack and with this in his hand returned to the kittens.

There were five, and he noticed their tigerish markings without comprehending as, one by one, he caught them and thrust them into the bag. They were old enough to struggle, spitting, clawing and biting at his fingers.

Throwing the bag over his shoulder he stumped down the hill to the burn, stopping twice on the way to wipe the sweat that trickled down his face and neck, rising in beads between the roots of his lint-white hair.

Behind him, the buildings of the farm-steading shimmered in the heat. The few trees on the slope raised dry, brittle branches towards a sky bleached almost white. The smell of the farm, mingled with peat-reek, dung, cattle, milk, and the dark tang of the soil, was strong in his nostrils, and when he halted there was no sound but his own breathing and the liquid burbling of the burn.

Throwing the sack on the bank, he stepped into the stream. The water was low, and grasping a great boulder in the bed of the burn he strained to lift it, intending to make a pool.

He felt no reluctance at performing the execution. He had no feelings about the matter. He had drowned kittens before. He would drown them again.

Panting with his exertion, the hired man cupped water between his hands and dashed it over his face and neck in a glistening shower. Then he turned to the sack and its prisoners.

He was in time to catch the second kitten as it struggled out of the bag. Thrusting it back and twisting the mouth of the sack close, he went after the other. Hurrying on the sun-browned grass, treacherous as ice, he slipped and fell headlong but grasped the runaway in his outflung hand.

It writhed round immediately and sank needle-sharp teeth into his thumb so that he grunted with pain and shook it from him. Unhurt, it fell by a clump of whins and took cover beneath them.

The hired man, his stolidity shaken by frustration tried to follow. The whins were thick and, scratched for his pains, he drew back, swearing flatly, without colour or passion.

Stooping, he could see the eyes of the kitten staring at him from the shadows under the whins. Its back was arched, its fur erect, its mouth open, and its thin lips drawn back over its tiny white teeth.

The hired man saw, again without understanding, the beginnings of tufts on the flattened ears. In his dull mind he felt a dark resentment at this creature which defied him. Rising, he passed his hand up his face in heavy thought, then slithering down to the stream, he began to gather stones. With an armful of small water-washed pebbles he returned to the whins.

First he strove to strike at the kitten from above. The roof of the whins was matted and resilient. The stones could not penetrate it. He flung straight then – to maim or kill – but the angle was difficult and only one missile reached its mark, rebounding from the ground and striking the kitten a glancing blow on the shoulder.

Kneeling, his last stone gone, the hired man watched, the red in his face deepening and thin threads of crimson rising in the whites of his eyes as the blood mounted to his head. A red glow of anger was spreading through his brain. His mouth worked and twisted to an ugly rent.

'Wait – wait,' he cried hoarsely, and, turning, ran heavily up the slope to the trees. He swung his whole weight on a low-hanging branch, snapping it off with a crack like a gunshot.

Seated on the warm, short turf, the hired man prepared his weapon, paring at the end of the branch till the point was sharp as a dagger. When it was ready he knelt on his left knee and swung the branch to find the balance. The kitten was almost caught.

The savage lance-thrust would have skewered its body as a trout is spiked on the beak of a heron, but the point, slung too low, caught in a fibrous root and snapped off short. Impotently the man jabbed with his broken weapon while the kitten retreated disdainfully to the opposite fringe of the whins.

In the slow-moving mind of the hired man the need to destroy the kitten had become an obsession. Intent on this victim, he forgot the others abandoned by the burn side; forgot the passage of time, and the hard labour of the day behind him. The kitten, in his distorted mind, had grown to a monstrous thing, centring all the frustrations of a brutish existence. He craved to kill ...

But so far the honours lay with the antagonist.

In a sudden flash of fury the man made a second bodily assault on the whins and a second time retired defeated.

He sat down on the grass to consider the next move as the first breath of the breeze wandered up the hill. As though that were the signal, in the last moments of the sun, a lark rose, close at hand, and mounted the sky on the flood of its own melody.

The man drank in the coolness thankfully, and, taking a pipe from his pocket, lit the embers of tobacco in the bowl. He flung the match from him, still alight, and a dragon's tongue of amber flame ran over the dry grass before the breeze, reached a bare patch of sand and flickered out. Watching it, the hired man knitted his brows and remembered the heather-burning, and mountain hares that ran before the scarlet terror. And he looked at the whins.

The first match blew out in the freshening wind, but at the second the bush burst into crackling flame.

The whims were alight on the leeward side and burned slowly against the wind. Smoke rose thickly, and sparks and lighted shivers of wood sailed off on the wind to light new fires on the grass of the hillside.

Coughing as the pungent smoke entered his lungs, the man circled the clump till the fire was between him and the farm. He could see the kitten giving ground slowly before the flame. He thought for a moment of lighting this side of the clump also and trapping it between two fires; took his matches from his pocket, hesitated, and replaced them. He could wait.

Slowly, very slowly, the kitten backed towards him. The wind fought for it, delaying, almost holding the advance of the fire through the whins.

Showers of sparks leaped up from the bushes that crackled and spluttered as they burned, but louder than the crackling of the whims, from the farm on the slope of the hill, came another noise – the clamour of voices. The hired man walked clear of the smoke that obscured his view and stared up the hill.

The thatch of the farmhouse, dry as tinder, was aflare.

Gaping, he saw the flames spread to the roof of the byre, to the stables; saw the farmer running the horses to safety, and heard the thunder of hooves as the scared cattle, turned loose, rushed from the yard. He saw a roof collapse in an uprush of smoke and sparks, while a kitten, whose sire was a wild cat, passed out of the whins unnoticed and took refuge in a deserted burrow.

From there, with cold, defiant eyes, it regarded the hired man steadfastly.

Alexander Reid

10

The Country Girls

The convent was a grey stone building with hundreds of small square curtainless windows like so many eyes spying out on the wet sinful town. There were green railings round it and high green gates that led to a dark cypress avenue. My father got out of the car to open the gates, and gave the door a god-awful bang. Mr Brennan winced and I was ashamed that my father didn't know better.

We parked the car under a tree and got out. We went down a flight of stone steps and crossed a concrete yard towards an open door. In the hallway a nun came forward to meet us. She wore a black, loose-fitting habit and a black veil over her head. Framing her face, and covering her forehead, her ears, and her chest was a stiff white thing which they call a gamp. It almost covered her eyebrows but you could just barely see the tips of them. They were black and they met in the middle over the bridge of her red nose. Her face was shiny.

My father took off his hat and told her who we were. Mr Brennan followed in with the cases.

'You're welcome,' she said to Baba and myself. Her hand was cold.

'Well, Baba, try to behave yourself,' Mr Brennan said doubtfully to Baba. Martha kissed me and put two coins into my hand. I said 'Oh no,' but as I was saying it my fingers closed over them gratefully. Reluctantly I kissed my father and I clung for a second to Mr Brennan and tried to thank him but I was too embarrassed.

The nun smiled all through her farewells. She had been watching others since early morning.

'They will settle down,' she said. Her voice was determined though not harsh; but when she said 'They will settle down' she seemed to be saying 'They must settle down.'

Our parents left. I thought of them going off to have tea and mixed grill in the warm hotel and I could taste the hot pepper taste of Yorkshire relish.

'Well now,' said the nun, taking a man's silver watch out of her pocket. 'First your tea. Follow me,' and we followed her down a long hallway. It had red tiles on the floor and there were shiny white tiles half-way up the walls. On each tiled window-ledge there was a castor-oil plant and at the bottom of the hall there was a row of oak presses. It was like a hospital, but it smelt of wax polish instead of anaesthetics. It was scrupulously and frighteningly clean. Dirt can be consoling and friendly in a strange place, I thought.

We hung our coats in the cloakroom and she helped us find a compartment in the press where our names were already written and where we were to store caps, gloves, shoes, boot polish, prayer-books, and small things like that. The press was like a honeycomb and not all the compartments were filled yet.

We followed her across another concrete yard to the refectory. She walked busily and the thick black rosary beads, hanging from her waist, swung outwards as she walked. We went into a big room with a high ceiling and long wooden tables stretching lengthwise. There were benches at either side of the tables.

The big girls, or the 'senior' girls, sat at one table and they were talking furiously. Talking about the holidays and the times they had. I suppose a lot of them were inventing things that never happened, just to make themselves important. Most of them had their hair freshly washed and one or two were very pretty. I picked out the pretty ones at once. At the junior table the new girls were strangers to one another. They looked lost and mopey, and cried quietly to themselves.

We were put sitting opposite one another and Baba smiled across at me, but we still hadn't spoken. A little nun poured us two cups of tea from a big white enamel tea-pot. She was so small I thought she'd drop the teapot. She wore a white muslin apron over her black habit. The apron meant that she was a lay nun. The lay nuns did the cooking and cleaning and scrubbing; and they were lay nuns because they had no money or no education when they entered the convent. The other nuns were called choir nuns. I didn't know that then but one of the senior girls explained it to me. Her name was Cynthia and she taught me a lot of things.

The bread was already buttered and a dopey girl next to me kept passing me a plate of dull grey bread.

*   *   *

We went to bed early.

Our dormitory was on the first floor. There was a lavatory on the landing outside it, and twenty or thirty girls were queueing there, hopping from one foot to another as if they couldn't wait. I took off my shoes and carried them into the dormitory. It was a long room with windows on either side, and a door at the far end. Over the door was a large crucifix, and there were holy pictures along the yellow distempered walls. There were two rows of iron beds down the length of the room. They were covered with white cotton counterpanes and the iron was painted white as well. The beds were numbered and I found mine easily enough. Baba was six beds away from me. At least it was nice to know that she was near, in case we should ever speak. There were three radiators along the wall but they were cold.

I sat down on the chair beside my bed, took off my garters, and peeled my stockings off slowly. The garters were too tight and they had made marks on my legs. I was looking at the red marks, worrying in case I'd have varicose veins before morning; and I didn't know that Sister Margaret was standing right behind me. She wore rubber-soled shoes and she had a way of stealing up on one. I jumped off the chair when she said, 'Now, girls.' I turned round to face her. Her eyes were cross and I could see a small cist on one of her irises. She was that near to me.

'The new girls won't know this, but our convent has always been proud of its modesty. Our girls, above anything else, are good and wholesome and modest. One expression of modesty is the way a girl dresses and undresses. She should do so with decorum and modesty. In an open dormitory like this ...' she paused, because someone had come in the bottom door and had bashed a ewer against the woodwork. Even my ear-lobes were blushing. She went on: 'Upstairs the senior girls have separate cubicles; but, as I say, in an open dormitory like this, girls are requested to dress and undress under the shelter of their dressing-gowns. Girls should face the foot of the bed, doing this, as they might surprise each other if they face the side of the bed.' She coughed and went off twiddling a bunch of keys in the air. She unlocked the oak door at the end of the room and went inside.

The girl allotted to the bed next to mine raised her eyes to heaven. She had squint eyes and I didn't like her. Not because of the squint but because she looked like someone who would have bad taste about everything. She was wearing a pretty, expensive dressing-gown and rich fluffy slippers; but you felt that she bought them to show off, and not because they were pretty. I saw her put two bars of chocolate under her pillow.

Trying to undress under a dressing-gown is a talent you must develop. Mine fell off six or seven times, but finally I managed to keep it on by stooping very low.

I was rooting in my travel-bag when the lights went out. Small figures in nightdresses hurried up the carpeted passage and disappeared into the cold white beds.

I wanted to get the cake that was in the bottom of my bag. The tea-service was on top, so I took it out piece by piece. Baba crept up to the foot of my bed and for the first time we talked, or rather, we whispered.

'Jesus, 'tis hell,' she said. 'I won't stick it for a week.'

'Nor me. Are you hungry?'

'I'd eat a young child,' she said. I was just getting my nail-file out of my toilet-bag, to cut a hunk of cake with, when the key was turned in the door at the end of the room. I covered the cake quickly with a towel and we stood there perfectly still, as Sister Margaret came towards us, holding her flash-lamp.

'What is the meaning of this?' she asked. She knew our names already and addressed us by our full names, not just Bridget (Baba's real name) and Caithleen; but Bridget Brennan and Caithleen Brady.

'We were lonely, Sister,' I said.

'You are not alone in your loneliness. Loneliness is no excuse for disobedience.' She was speaking in a penetrating whisper. The whole dormitory could hear her.

'Go back to your bed, Bridget Brennan,' she said. Baba tripped off quietly. Sister Margaret shone the flash-lamp to and fro, until the beam caught the little tea-service on the bed.

'What is this?' she asked, picking up one of the cups.

'A tea-service, Sister. I brought it because my mother died.' It was a stupid thing to say and I regretted it at once. I'm always saying stupid things, because I don't think before I say them.

'Sentimental childish conduct,' she said. She lifted the outside layer of her black habit and shaped it into a basket. Then she put the tea-service in there and carried it off.

I got in between the icy sheets and ate a piece of seed cake. The whole dormitory was crying. You could hear the sobbing and choking under the covers. Smothered crying.

The head of my bed backed on to the head of another girl's bed; and in the dark a hand came through the rungs and put a bun on my pillow. It was an iced bun and there was something on top of the icing. Possibly a cherry. I gave her a piece of cake and we shook hands. I wondered what she looked like, as I hadn't noticed her when the lights were on. She was a nice girl whoever she was. The bun was nice too. Two or three beds away I heard some girl munch an apple under the covers. Everyone seemed to be eating and crying for their mothers.

My bed faced a window and I could see a sprinkling of stars in one small corner of the sky. It was nice to lie there watching the stars, waiting for them to fade or to go out, or to flare up into one brilliant firework. Waiting for something to happen in the deathly, unhappy silence.

Edna O'Brien
Abridged

11

Pakistani

She was a quiet child.

She stood there, in a corner of the grey playground, and watched – watched out of those dark eyes, timidly, as if she were afraid of being hurt. The other children, shouting, screaming, laughing, kicking, created a wave of violent, splendid motion before her; and as she watched, she longed to be a part of the wave, to be hurled among them, dashed from one moment of exhilaration to the next, and finally to be drowned in an ecstasy of movement.

She stood quite still, and watched. And the children, because they knew she was watching, shouted more gaily, screamed more shrilly. Deafened by the noise, hypnotised by the motion, she felt her limbs becoming heavier and heavier, weighing her down so that she was clamped to the spot, an island in a foaming sea. She prayed. She prayed to her own private god. 'Oh please, please let them speak to me. Please let them like me.'

'You're the New Girl.'

It was a statement of fact, a child's introduction. And she acknowledged it thankfully.

'Yes.'

The girl who stood before her was short and plump, with round glasses and wispy brown hair. They examined one another for a moment. The girl with brown hair shifted from one foot to the other, and rubbed the back of her leg with her toe.

'Why are you wearing trousers.'

'I just do. They're not trousers, they're Shalwar.'

'Oh ... Do you want to play? I'll let you play with me.'

And so she became a part of them, shrieking with the rest. She was one of the great struggling mass of kicking legs, and waving arms, and streaming hair, and gaping, laughing mouths. Her soul lifted in a moment of bliss, and she knew the sensation of complete self-forgetfulness, of being a thousand people and not one.

'You kicked me.' It was the girl with brown hair, standing before her, pink with indignation.

'I – I didn't mean to.'

The girl with brown hair had been kicked by several people without thinking twice of it. But there was something about the

manner of the new girl – a fearfulness, a stillness – which gave her, somehow, an odd sensation of power.

'You kicked me! Darkie, you kicked me! Darkie, Darkie; Pakistani!'

Suddenly everyone was giggling, and chanting, and pointing 'Darkie, Darkie, Darkie' in a crescendo of sound, and at the climax came the shattering scream 'Pakistani!' Then again. And again. Waving arms. Gaping, shrieking mouths ...

She stood quite still, then turned and walked away. And they did not see – no one saw – the hot tears that burned into her cheeks, into her memory, nor the fire which branded her soul. Why? Why? Why am I Pakistani? Why me? 'Pakistani!' They meant it as a terrible insult. But it was her country. Her parents had taught her to love it. God, Parents and Country. That was what they had taught her, and she loved them all. But she loved these people too, she loved this country. The screaming children did not touch that love, because it was something higher than them. She had this tremendous, aching love inside her, a love which was closely connected with the pain of the hurling insults. Some day she would show them. Some day she would teach them to respect her country, and themselves. She would teach them her love.

The girl with brown hair, withdrawn now from the shouting children, watched her, with a kind of fear.

The Pakistani girl was standing, quite still in the middle of the playground. And she was smiling.

12

Clinging to the Wreckage

At the beginning, when I was away at school, I was extremely lonely. Loneliness, however, the birthright of the only child, held no particular terrors for me. In the holidays, having built his new house near to our old country cottage, my father devoted almost all his spare time to a large garden, and as his eyes failed and the flowers and vegetables faded from his view, his gardening became more dedicated, until, when he could no longer see the results of his labours, but had to rely on my mother or me to describe the health of a dahlia or the wilt of a clematis, he spent every possible hour pricking out, or potting on, or groping for dead heads and trying to get a correct aim with his secateurs. He never welcomed visitors and would often ask my mother to lead him away into the undergrowth if they appeared at the gate, so a month or so would pass without our seeing anyone at all. My segregated education seemed to have driven some sort of wedge between me and Iris and the Mullard boys, so holidays were a solitary pleasure which I tried to carry on at school.

Being alone was easier, I had long ago discovered, if you became two people, the actor and the observer. The observer was always the same, the actor played many parts: an officer in the Foreign Legion, for instance, or a ruthless private detective with rooms in Half Moon Street, or a Brigadier in Napoleon's army. 'There he goes,' I was able to say about myself, even in the deeply unhappy days when I lolloped about a frozen football field, keeping as far as possible from the ball, 'cantering across the burning sands with his crack platoon of Spahis (ex-murderers, robbers and at least one Duke disappointed in love, but whoever asked questions of a Legionnaire?) in search of the tents of Mahmoud Bey, and a levelling of the score after the disgrace of Sidi Ben Oud.' Later my character became more sophisticated, as I came more under the influence of Noël Coward and Dornford Yates.

'*Sic vos non vobis mellificatis apes*. Translate, Mortimer.'

'Thus you don't make honey for yourselves, you apes, sir.' Mortimer drew a flat gold cigarette-case from the breast pocket of his immaculate grey, double-breasted jacket. He was bubbling with suppressed laughter: the answer had been deliber-

ately misleading. With a tap the heavy case sprang open and he offered it to the bewildered little man at the blackboard. 'Turkish this side,' he said, 'and Virginian the other.'

Later still, when I made a friend, we inflicted our lies on each other. Childhood is a great time for lying. Later in life you may be able to boast of some real achievement or some extraordinary adventure, in childhood all must be supplied from the imagination. So I told my friend that I was the son of a Russian aristocrat, smuggled out of Moscow during the revolution, and had been kindly taken in by the simple English lawyer with whom I happened to live. I had a long story, a rare sporting fantasy, about walking along the towpath at Hammersmith when the cox of the Oxford crew had a heart attack and, being then of the appropriate weight, steering the eight to victory in the Boat Race. More consistently, I pretended that my parents never stopped going to cocktail parties, bickering, throwing 'White Ladies' and 'Manhattans' into each other's faces and would soon be getting a divorce. If I had one clear ambition during those years it was to be the child of a broken home.

John Mortimer

13

How Many Miles to Babylon?

As a child I was alone. I am making no excuses for myself, merely stating a fact. I was isolated from the surrounding children of my own age by the traditional barriers of class and education. Not that I was educated in any formal way. A series of ladies taught me a series of subjects until at the magic age of ten I was handed over to the curate who, presumably to supplement his tiny income, spent several hours each day trying to teach me mathematics, English literature, a smattering of French grammar, and of course Latin. Latin was his subject and his face would begin to glow with pleasure as the moment arrived for us to open up one of the numerous books we translated together. On days when I felt particularly unkind I would fumble and stumble over the words and watch maliciously the visible disintegration of his pleasure. He smelt delicately of peppermints. Once every hour or so two of his white fingers would probe into his waistcoat pocket and pull out the small white sweet which he would slip into his mouth almost as if he were performing some minor criminal act.

There was also the piano teacher who used to come down once a week on the train from Dublin. I remember little about him except for his ineffectiveness as a teacher and the reason for his going. My mother would come into the drawing-room towards the end of each lesson and sigh restlessly from her chair, fretted by my lack of progress. He was a nervous man who became almost insane in her presence. His hands would shake, and he would begin to tear distractedly at the dark stains of hardened food that decorated the front of his jacket as he watched me play. The drawing-room smelt of applewood and turf, and, in the autumn, the bitter end-of-the-year smell of chrysanthemums which stood in pots massed in one of the deep bay windows, shades of yellow, gold, bronze and white, like a second fire in the room. The black ebony case of the Steinway grand reflected the flowers. The music teacher was ridiculously out of place.

He rose and approached my mother, bowing at her as he crossed the floor. Masses of golden birds flew in gigantic curves on the blue carpet under his sad shoes. It must have been autumn because the smell of the flowers and his words are tangled together in my mind.

'Yes. Ah yes. He comes along very nicely ... the little fellow. You do notice ... yes ... progress ... I feel. I do hope you are being ...'

His faded eyes twitched as he spoke. His finger picked and picked. Soon, I thought silently, there will be a hole.

'... satisfied.' He bent low over her as he spoke the word. She moved her head slightly away from him.

'Oh, yes. Progress. Of a kind, I suppose.'

She waved him away with her hand, and he straightened up. I sat at the piano unmoving. I had developed the technique of listening to a fine art. I could become at will as still and invisible as a chair or a bowl of flowers.

'Such a deal of your talent, Mrs Moore, has rubbed off on the ... um ... little fellow.'

Overcome suddenly by the thought of the stains, he spread his grey long fingers out over the front of his coat, like two very dead starfish on a beach. I played an arpeggio softly and my mother waved her hand towards the door.

'Your train, Mr Cave. I mean you mustn't miss ...'

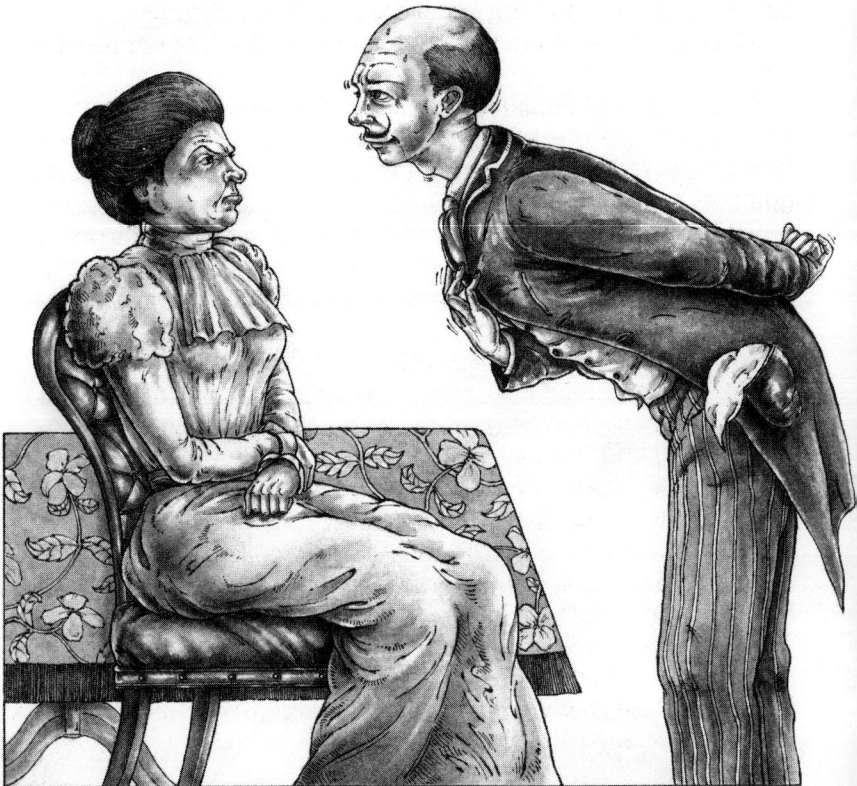

'No. No. Of course not. Well...' He paused and looked around the room as if he were trying to memorise it for use during his darker days. 'I'll be on my way so. Time and ... oh ha ... trains wait for no man.'

He bowed once more to my mother. She smiled with her lips, but her eyes passed him by. He turned to me.

'And you, young fellamelad... till Tuesday. Mind you practise now.'

He moved towards the door. Suddenly I felt some sort of emotion towards him. I no longer remember what it was, and I slipped off the chair and followed him out of the room and across the dark back hall. In the semi-darkness he reached out with a hand and squeezed my shoulder gently.

'Such a beautiful woman, God love her. So ...' Words failed him.

'What a lucky little fellamelad you are to have a beautiful mammy like that.'

'Have you a coat?'

I pulled with both hands at the brass door-knob and the door came open letting in the east wind. Some letters fluttered on the long mahogany table, and shocked flames twisted for a moment out of the grate and then recovered their equilibrium.

'Coat? No coat, sonny.' He gave a little laugh. 'I never feel the cold.'

A lie, I thought. He was a man, I'd have said, who had never felt warm in his life, or well, or momentarily gay. He stepped bravely out into the evening, and bowed once more before going down the steps.

Father was in the drawing-room when I got back. I stood in the embrasure just outside the door and listened to their voices.

'... But go he must. I simply can't bear the thought of having him in the house any more.'

'My dear Alicia, you are absurd.'

'No. Not remotely.'

'But what can I say?'

'An excuse. You must be able to think of something. Anything. He has such an appalling smell.'

'I can hardly say that. Come now.'

I could hear her skirts swish as she moved across the room.

'He must be ill. Some terrible disease. I get the feeling he's leaving it lying around all over the place.'

She opened the window and the wind rattled in.

'He's like someone who's been eaten by life and there's nothing left but this terrible smell ... More, more air.'

Another window sighed open.

'He's a good teacher. You said so yourself.'

'Frederick, I can't abide him in this house any more. I can't speak more plainly. I shall teach the child myself.'

There was a very long silence. My father's face would show little emotion. His voice would show little emotion, but there were times when he would twist his hands together in a gesture of incredible violence. Mother never appeared to notice, or if she did it was of no interest to her.

'Dragging his disease and poverty into my drawing-room. You will write, won't you.' It was a command rather than a question. I heard a quick sigh from father.

'If you insist.'

'Oh but I do.'

The piano teacher never appeared again. My mother became bored or exasperated quite soon by the clumsiness of my fingers and after a while the piano lessons ceased.

*   *   *

Jerry was around always. The stable-yard was where he was always to be seen. He had a neat facility for keeping out of the way of the horses' hooves and the fists of the more quick-tempered men. I noticed his feet before his face. In the summer they were bare, dust-grey and with soles obviously as hard and impervious to stones, thorns, damp, as were the soles of my expensive black leather shoes. In the winter he moved awkwardly in a pair of men's boots tied on to him with string. We never spoke, barely even nodded, and yet I knew that he wasn't just there for the horses, he was as aware of me as he was of their polished perfection.

*   *   *

It was about early May when we spoke first. The daffodils were crumpling and shrinking. The weather had been warm and there had been a great surge of leaf growth, the chestnut candles were at their best. I stepped on to the grass from the darkness. There was a sudden noise from under the willow and a splash. My heart thudded with alarm. Down all the years I had been warned about gipsies. I moved with caution across the grass, now long enough to bend caressingly under my feet. At the foot of the tree was a pile of clothes. There was no other sign of life, no sound. I picked up the clothes and hid them away under a bush, then went to the edge of the water to wait for the trespasser.

'Come on in, why don't you?'

A voice shouted from quite far out in the lake. He started to swim towards me and I recognised the shining, grinning face to be Jerry.

I waited until he was standing waist-deep in water just below me before speaking.

'Don't you know this is private property?'

He spat into the water. It wasn't aggressive in any way, merely contemptuous. The blob of spit floated slowly away.

'You're trespassing.'

'Well?'

'I could have you prosecuted.'

'Well, why don't you?'

I felt somewhat foolish. He looked at me for a long time with clear, bright blue eyes rimmed with pink. He had perhaps been staying up too late or possibly crying. I didn't think he looked like someone who cried.

'There's lots of room for both of us,' he said finally. 'Come on in.'

I pondered. He turned away and dived under the water. When he came up he was about twenty yards out. He waved at me. Sparks of water flew from his arm. I took off my clothes and slid down the grass into the water.

It was more fun swimming with someone else, there was no doubt about that.

*   *   *

He held out his hand towards me and I clasped it. We lay and looked at the forbidden sun until it moved behind the trees and the wind started to worry us.

I had a friend. A private and secret friend. I never went to his house nor he to mine. We met, either down by the lake, or up on the hill behind the house where I would take my pony in the afternoons when he had finished school. Up there hidden satisfactorily by a ridge of shining granite we built ourselves a riding school. We moved stones and filled in holes to make a track round the whin bushes, and we built half a dozen light jumps. It seemed perfect to us. After his lesson I would let Pharaoh loose to crop what grass he could and we would crouch in the shelter of a stone wall and work at Jerry's homework.

*   *   *

Jerry carried round with him a mouth organ, on which he was able to play with great virtuosity. He would squat down to play,

with his eyes shut and his cupped hands pressed up against his mouth. His bare toes would wriggle on the ground in a sort of ecstatic dance of their own. He played ballads, both sentimental and revolutionary, and ancient wordless tunes of almost oriental complication. Sometimes I would try to sing the words that he would throw to me out of the corner of his mouth. I learnt a lot of history that might have alarmed Mr Bingham. Most times I would just lie in content and listen. When we fought he always won, though as time went on I became a more practical fighter than I had been before. I learnt some tricks, short cuts. On horseback I had the edge over him as far as style was concerned. My style was almost impeccable, his, non-existent, nor did he appreciate the need for such a nicety. But, style or no style, he had no trouble in making my Pharaoh go. Looking back it all seems idyllic, but I'm sure that we had our ugly moments as well as our beautiful ones. Real friendship admits recognition of the ugly as well as the beautiful. I remember the moments that snatched me from the passive solitude of my normal life, warned me of the pleasure and the fear of living.

*   *   *

'I'll be leaving school in June.'

We were lying on top of a hill watching a man and his horse ploughing a long strip of a field below us. The horse's head drooped forward as if it were completely relaxed, its huge white feathered hooves never lost their rhythm for a moment. The man was smoking a pipe and a streamer of smoke trailed behind him as he moved. The perfection of the deep straight lines spread.

'Why?'

'What do you mean, why, you omadhan? Because I have to.'

I turned my eyes from the ploughers and looked at Jerry.

'But you're only the same age as I am. I mean a child. We're children yet.'

He punched me on the side of the head.

'I'll not be a child much longer. Then you'll have to watch your step when you're with me, and your lip.'

'What'll you do?'

He nodded down towards the man with the horse.

'That, I suppose. Find some eejit to employ me. There's nothing to do at home but plant the spuds and then dig them up and eat them. I've been doing that for years anyroad. She milks the cow.' He pondered for a moment or two. 'I might run away with the tinkers.'

He didn't sound as if he meant it so I paid no attention to what sounded to me like a most romantic notion.

'She wants me to join the army.' He spat, as always, unnervingly close to me. I twitched rather than moved my leg. 'Follow me dad. Then she'd have two envelopes arriving. On the pig's bloody back.'

'You could play your mouth organ in the army band.'

'Thanks a lot. I'd rather stay at home. I don't feel I'm cut out to be a soldier. Perhaps I love myself too much.'

'Look, Jerry ...'

'Mmmm.'

He was pulling a grass stalk in and out of a gap between his two front teeth.

'Why don't you try and get a job here? In the stables. You'd like that, wouldn't you?'

He shook his head.

'It passed through my mind.'

'But why not? It seems like a great idea to me.'

'Well, for one thing we wouldn't be able to be friends any more.'

Small brisk cries came up from the man ploughing. The horse moved faster, his head now straining forward.

'I don't see that.'

'I'd be working for you. It would be different.'

'Not for me, you blithering idiot.'

'Your father, you. It's all one. They wouldn't let us be friends.'

'Why should they care?'

Yet I knew they would care. He was right. My mother's mouth would purse up with disapproval, her voice rise alarmingly as it sometimes did when she spoke to my father.

'Why is neither here nor there. Your lot would care. My lot too if it came to it. One's as bad as the other.

* * *

He went, when the time came, to work for one of the local farmers, a tenant of my father, and we were able to meet less often. My life didn't seem to change at all. I grew. At times I was growing so fast that I imagined as I lay in bed at night that I could actually feel myself stretching between the smooth sheets. When it came to growing I left Jerry in the halfpenny place. His finger-nails became engrained with mud and he took to smoking. He would get strands of tobacco stuck on his tongue and would pinch them off between his thumb and forefinger with a gesture I had seen men in the yard use. It put years on his age, or so I thought. Like he had said, he no longer seemed to be a child. He earned the amazing sum of seven shillings and sixpence a week. In spite of the fact that his mother took all but a shilling of it, no Rothschild could have ever enjoyed their money more. We would crouch for hours over the racing page in the paper and with enormous pleasure win and lose hypothetical fortunes.

* * *

It was discovered. I don't know how, but I had a feeling at the time that Mr Bingham the ex-ear puller had something to do with it. Maybe it was simply that as time passed we became careless, rode the ponies in view of the house, or laughed too loud at our own bad jokes, whatever it was it came to my mother's ears.

Jennifer Johnston
Abridged

46

14

Comfort Herself

The pattern of the days changed when school broke up and the children came down the middle of the lane singing,

'No more Latin, no more French
No more sitting on a hard old bench,'

as loud as they could, waving their drawings and swinging their school bags round their head.

'Six weeks of dreadful racket,' Granny sighed. 'And that ridiculous song when they don't even learn French, let alone Latin.'

'Traditional,' Grandad said. 'It's what their parents sang.' The children had stopped outside the cottage and Lettie walked up the brick path and knocked on the front door.

'Can *she* come out to play?' Lettie said jerking her head towards Comfort. She carried a pile of old exercise books in her arms and her green eyes were bold in her hot pink face, ready for anything. Hadn't she just finished six years at Penfold School where Miss Slade and Mrs Arthur both had their knives into her?

'I don't really see any necessity....' Granny began but catching sight of Comfort at the kitchen door with her face forlorn and her hands all floury, she relented. 'Oh, go out and play, child, but no screaming, mind.'

'Course not,' Lettie said primly and Comfort followed her down the path and across the grass which was cut short now and dried in the sun like yellow dog fur. Some twenty children were waiting under the copper beech trees and Comfort smiled carefully.

'It's *her*,' Lettie's little brother, Bobby, whispered, jigging up and down. 'She's coming out to play.'

'Who? What's she want to come out for?' Betty said sulkily. She was almost nine and working hard to be Lettie's best friend.

'The black girl. She's coming out to play with us,' Bobby hiss-whispered.

'You shut up, you,' Lettie said cuffing his head which was something she did quite often. 'Who you calling black, showing your ignorance? You want your mouth washed out with soap, you do.'

'I'm telling Mum, you wait,' Bobby gulped but he did not go. The others spread out in a circle round her, blue eyes, green eyes, grey eyes, brown eyes staring. Comfort was used to staring but these eyes seemed different, gentler, as if they had taken their colour from the sky, grass, earth and water of the marsh itself.

'Stop staring, stop being rude,' Lettie said, ashamed at the unsophisticated way that her group was behaving. 'You get them everywhere nowadays, people like her. Don't you ever watch the telly? What are we all going to play then?'

'Grandmother's footsteps,' Bobby said, wisely selecting a game in which older ones did not have all the advantage.

'Does *she* know Grandmother's footsteps?' Betty nodded towards Comfort. 'They might not have it where she comes from.'

'I come from London,' Comfort said still smiling. You always had to smile till your cheeks ached in a new place. There were rules people told you and rules you had to find out for yourself.

'I'll be Grandmother if you like?' Lettie said and nobody argued though they muttered a bit when Lettie kept turning round and shouting everybody back except Comfort. What kind of Grandmother would Comfort be, everybody wondered and Comfort wondered too, lenient or strict, sending back people if they breathed even. She had been like that in Shepherds Bush one time, Clapham, too, but it wouldn't be right when she was new in Penfold. She didn't stay Grandmother long and it was

Lettie she allowed to touch her shoulder first. One or two shouted 'Not fair,' but they went on playing just the same. They left for their dinners and came back for a game of kick-the-can because Lettie ruled in Penfold, okay, and a new girl in the village was exciting.

'I'm all out of puff with these kids' games,' Lettie said dropping down in the grass.

'Me too,' Comfort said dropping beside her.

'Where do you come from then?' Betty asked looping back her hair and fastening her blue butterfly slide.

'London,' Comfort said. 'I was born in London. My mum and me always lived in London.'

'You English then?' Lettie said, her round green eyes rolled thoughtfully towards Comfort.

'Well, I'm half-English, half-Ghanaian,' Comfort said.

'Half-Ghanaian? What's that when it's at home?' Betty said raising a titter from the other children.

'Oh, buzz off, you lot,' Lettie said impatiently. 'What you want to hang round us for all the time?'

'Bossy knickers, village green don't belong to you, Lettie Stamp,' Betty said. She and the others gathered disconsolately at the edge of the green and waited, preferring Lettie's tyrannies to the dullness of playing without her.

'Let's get shot of the little kids, shall we?' Lettie said putting her arm round Comfort's shoulders and steering her across the lane and through the churchyard gate. 'You're not allowed in the churchyard,' she shouted threateningly when the others tried to follow. 'Rector'll catch you and then you'll cop it.'

'Are *we* allowed then?' Comfort said anxiously as Lettie lead her round the back of the church.

'Course we are, leastways you're allowed if you're with me,' Lettie said. 'I'm in the choir, and my great-granny only died three months back, so I'm allowed in to put flowers on her grave, see, so I'm twice allowed.' Even so Lettie felt suddenly shy, she picked a few moon-daisies from the long grass and filled a glass jar from a tap fixed to the church wall until it passed off. She had longed for a friend of her own age all her life, prayed to God every night and now there was this black girl and the village agog. Lettie didn't know whether to laugh or cry.

'You can sit on my great-granny's grave if you like,' Lettie said extending her arm to the marble edge in hostess style. 'Grass might be damp.'

'Thanks,' said Comfort. There was a headstone made of speckly imitation marble with *Letitia Stamp* and the date of her birth and death in gold-filled letters and lots of bright green chips like bath salts.

'Saves weeding, saves cutting the grass,' Lettie explained flattening the green chips with the palm of her hand to accommodate the jar of moon daisies. 'My great-granny went to school in a white pinny, same school,' she nodded her head towards the deserted building. 'We got this photo, *Letitia* same as me,' her eyes turned to Comfort curiously. 'Where are your great-grannies then? You got four, everybody has.'

'Well, there's one in Harrogate, I think,' Comfort said startled by the question and feeling it shameful not to know for certain but nobody had ever talked to her of great-grandmothers. There must be two in Africa. She could imagine them if she tried, *dream-see* Carmen called it, buried close to the sea, sand and little dusty plants like sea-holly and palm trees above. It would be nice to really *know* your great-grannies had been to the same school as you and were safe in the earth beneath you. That was roots. You would really belong to Penfold then.

'Did you like that school?' Comfort asked.

'Blooming awful, same teachers first to last,' Lettie said fiercely. 'I'm going to the big school next term, Dunton Wood Comprehensive, it's a fresh start my mum says.' Lettie sighed as if she didn't have much confidence in fresh starts. 'Brown blazers and yellow shirts. Are you going to Dunton Wood; be brilliant if you was going to Dunton Wood?'

Comfort shook her head. The back of the dark green cardigan was finished already, spread out on the sofa arm, knitted was warmer than shop bought and Folkestone could be bracing. 'Going to weekly boarding school in Folkestone.'

'Boarding school? Fancy a girl like you going to a boarding school?' Lettie's eyes were wide with amazement. 'All posh like Felicity Davis?'

'Who's she?' Comfort said.

'Mr and Mrs Davis are *only* the most important people in this village, that's all,' Lettie said astonished at such ignorance when Comfort had been in Penfold for at least two weeks. 'They *only* live in the Manor House and have the biggest farm on the marsh and their grandfather *only* planted the copper beeches on the green and they only have the bean-field where the whole village goes picking, that's all. Still I suppose you wouldn't know, would you, your granny being a foreigner?' Lettie added in a mollifying tone. 'Our Dad's cowman at Manor House Farm.'

'Foreigner?' Comfort said. 'My Granny's as English as English.'

'But she hasn't lived here long, you can't call two years long. Nearly all foreigners in the old cottages, foreigners aren't village, you can't call them village. Anyway wild horses wouldn't get me going to any blinking boarding school.' Lettie dusted the top of the headstone with the skirt of her dress. 'Still we can be brilliant friends for the holidays and weekends, can't we?'

'Okay then,' Comfort said.

'Want to see something magic? Lettie said running across to the railings. 'Woolly, Woolly,' she called into the field beyond. 'Come up, come up Woolly.' The flock of grazing sheep raised their heads uneasily and lumbered away but one large lamb trotted boldly towards Lettie's outstretched hand with its handful of long fresh grass.

'Magic, eh, my *sock* lamb?' Lettie looked back over her shoulder at Comfort's wide eyes, the balance between them restored. 'Lost his mother when he was born and now he thinks I'm his mother, see, because he slept in our kitchen and I gave him his bottle every day, didn't I, little Woolly? You can pat him if you like.' Comfort stretched her arm through the railings and patted the thick wool, springy dense and oily to the touch. Having a lamb which came when you called really did seem like magic.

*   *   *

'Can't we go to church?' Comfort said to Granny one Sunday. She could hardly get through the desert of the day, with Lettie

singing in the choir morning and evening and wanted at home to help with the roast and visiting aunts.

'We're not really churchy people,' Granny said pursing her lips and measuring the green cardigan sleeve against Comfort's arm. 'I don't need any church to tell me what's right, I think I do my duty.' It was her *duty* to care for Comfort, she thought, decreasing one stitch at the beginning of the row for the shoulder shaping. She would hardly have credited how fond she had grown of the child in spite of everything. Such feelings were almost a weakness at her time of life, a hostage given to fortune. Granny blew her nose vigorously and cast off one stitch at the end of the row.

'You don't go to church and you don't go bean-picking either,' Comfort said reproachfully because bean-picking looked like being a whole fortnight of desert Sundays. You could only go bean-picking with your own family, Lettie said, not altogether certain that Comfort could go with them. It depended on her granny who was quite a tartar and didn't care for people staring.

'Bean-picking? I should think not at our time of life,' Granny said. 'Pass me that wool.'

Later that evening Comfort wandered into the churchyard. It was after evensong and the church was quiet now, the red ball of the sun turning the grass to gold. Swallows gathered on the telegraph wires in long lines. They knew the days were shorter, Grandad said, they were getting ready to go to Africa. 'Come up, Woolly, come up, Woolly,' Comfort called softly and the sock lamb detached himself from the flock and came trotting to the gate taking the grass she offered. If it was magic Comfort had it too.

'What do you think you're blooming well doing?' Lettie shouted diving across the churchyard, pink with anger. 'You're not allowed in here unless you're with me. He's my lamb, Woolly is.' What a pity Lettie wasn't as pretty as her sister Auntie Em had said with the door not quite shut.

'Course I'm allowed,' Comfort said. 'Church belongs to everybody, Lettie Stamp.'

'I'm telling Rector. You don't even go to church and your granny doesn't either and she's a foreigner in this village and goodness knows what you are,' Lettie stomped up the lane.

'Course I do, I was born in England,' Comfort said stoutly. You had to stand up for yourself, Margaret said, don't let people trample you. But Lettie was angry. Would the Rector be angry too, going turkey-pink and shouting, Comfort wondered. She hated it when people got angry. It ended things, meant damage said and done which could never be undone. Like the night in Brixton. Suddenly the sound of crashing glass and people running and a white rexine chair leaping from a shop window and along the pavement as if by its own volition. There was glass all over the pavement next day, skittering under their feet like ice as they crossed to the taxi. She had been going to leave anyway, Margaret said.

Lettie was walking more slowly now and she stopped altogether at the rectory gate and began to pick a bunch of cow parsley for her rabbit. 'Want to see something funny?' she called presently.

'What?' said Comfort relief surging through her like warm water because they were friends again.

'You want to look through the windows then,' Lettie said nodding her head towards the school and turning down the lane. Comfort walked across the empty playground and jumped as high as she could, her fingers scrabbling at the gritty sill. For a few seconds she looked into the classroom, seeing small tables and chairs stacked upside down and paintings round the wall, a black face with round black eyes and a strip of yellow tee-shirt and gold earrings. Comfort landed back on the asphalt with a thump.

'Who says I look like that?' she demanded. Lettie had disappeared. The feelings whirled and fluctuated in Comfort's head like bonfire smoke on a windy day. The paintings certainly weren't beautiful. But how could you expect beautiful paintings from young kids. She was in the heads of all the children of Penfold School forever like Lettie's great-grandmother in her white pinny. 'Seven paintings of me on the school wall,' Comfort wrote in her diary that night. 'I've been painted by Dave, Ruth, Betty, Daisy, Lettie, Jim, Joy, Carol.' Whatever happened, everybody would remember her coming to the village. Granny and Grandad would always be foreigners but Comfort herself was part of Penfold.

Geraldine Kaye
Abridged

15

The Choosing

We were first equal Mary and I
with the same coloured ribbons in mouse-coloured hair
and with equal shyness,
we curtseyed to the lady councillor
for copies of Collins' Children's Classics.
First equal, equally proud.

Best friends too Mary and I
a common bond in being cleverest (equal)
in our small school's small class.
I remember
the competition for top desk
or to read aloud the lesson
at school service.
And my terrible fear
of her superiority at sums.

I remember the housing scheme
where we both stayed.
The same houses, different homes,
where the choices were made.

I don't know exactly why they moved,
but anyway they went.

Something about a three-apartment
and a cheaper rent.
But from the top deck of the high-school bus
I'd glimpse among the others on the corner
Mary's father, mufflered, contrasting strangely
with the elegant greyhounds by his side,
He didn't believe in high school education,
especially for girls,
or in forking out for uniforms.

Ten years later on a Saturday –
I am coming from the library –
sitting near me on the bus,
Mary
with a husband who is tall,
curly haired, has eyes
for no one else but Mary.
Her arms are round the full-shaped vase
that is her body.
Oh, you can see where the attraction lies
in Mary's life –
not that I envy her, really.

And I am coming from the library
with my arms full of books.
I think of those prizes that were ours for the taking
and wonder when the choices got made
we don't remember making.

Liz Lochhead

16
The Filleting Machine

Scene: *A council house living room, with kitchen off stage. The house is on the Ridges estate, North Shields. The area is a depressed enclave of poor whites who have been slum-cleared from the fish dock district. In the distance, the raucous strident sound of children in the battlefield of the street can be heard.* MA *is preparing a meal.* ALICE, *her daughter, is listening to a transistor radio. The kitchen door opens and* DAVY *comes cautiously in. He is dressed in a wind jacket and rubber boots. He begins to take off his jacket.* ALICE *studies him.*

ALICE: Where you been?

DAVY: Doon by.

ALICE: On the fish quay?

DAVY: So what?

ALICE: Get yor hammers if she finds out. Better hide them wellies.

DAVY *considers confiding a secret. He stands up holding his boots.*

DAVY: Gotta job.

ALICE: Gotta what?

DAVY: Gotta job.

ALICE: On the fish quay?

DAVY: Start o' Monday.

ALICE: Ye haven't?

DAVY: Wanna bet?

ALICE: Eee! what ye ganna tell Ma?

DAVY (*Doubtful*): Jus' tell her.

ALICE: She'll gan crackers.

DAVY: Who cares?

ALICE: She'll lose her blob.

DAVY (*Irritated*): Alreet! Alreet!

ALICE: What aboot yor interview for the Town Clerk's?

DAVY (*Contemptuous*): Oh! that! That's had it.

ALICE: Eee! She'll gan daft.

Offstage MA *can be heard returning. At the sound of his mother,* DAVY *panics, grabs his jacket and boots and prepares to bolt into the kitchen.*

DAVY: Now you shut yor gob, Alice, or A'll shut it for ye.

ALICE: Push off.

DAVY *retreats into the kitchen.* ALICE *turns up the radio and a second later* MA *comes in through the main door.*

MA: Alice! Torn that blarin' thing off. (MA *switches the radio off*) One row after another. (*From the kitchen comes the sound of a tap running.* MA *looks in the direction of the sound*) Is there somebody out there? Davy? Davy? Is that you son? (*She pauses, then shouting*) Davy?

DAVY: Aye, ma! (DAVY *comes in. He pushes past his mother, snatches the comic from his sister and sits*)

MA: Come on, bonny lad, it's past five o'clock. (*She sniffs inquiringly in the air*) Yor da wi' ye?

DAVY: No, ma.

MA: S'funny, could've swore A smelled him.

DAVY: Gotta lock in. Doon at Charlie's.

MA (*Outraged*): Gotta what? Has he had you in the boozer?

DAVY: Aw, ma! A'm ownly fifteen.

MA: An yor a big fifteen, an' yor da's a big idiot. Now come on, A want the truth.

DAVY: Jus' seen him gannin' in with his mates. Ye knaa! Chopper, Sainty, Danny Mac. Charlie gi' them a lock in.

MA: Mates! Bloody wasters more like it. Dissolvin' thor brains wi' broon ale. Three card brag 'till yon time. They'll take him ti the cleaners. Another short week. (*Suspiciously,* MA *sniffs again. She comes directly over to* DAVY *and bends over him*)

Poo! It's you, It's you, isn't it? Ye smell like a gut barrel. No
wonder A thought yor father was in the hoose.

DAVY: Aw, ma.

MA: Ye've been doon on that quay, haven't ye?

DAVY: Ma!

MA: Now come on, A want no lies.

DAVY: Just gi' me da a hand ti wash a few boxes oot. Gettim a
quick finish.

MA: A'll finish him.

DAVY: Bob Wilson give's a quid.

MA: Nivvor mind aboot Bob Wilson. Ye'll get the smell o' fish
on ye. Gans right thro' yor claes, into yor skin, an' thor's no
gettin' rid of it.

DAVY: Ma!

MA: Now, Davy, A've telled ye. (*She goes to the mantelpiece to
take a letter from an ornament. While her back is turned* ALICE
gestures to DAVY *urging him to tell his Ma about the job.* DAVY
summons up his courage)

DAVY: Ma! When A was on the quay....

MA: Now look, son, forget about the quay. Ye've got that interview next week. (*She demonstrates the letter*) This is your chance in life. Ye've got yor O-levels. Davy, it's yor chance ti mix wi better people.

DAVY: What's better aboot them?

MA: Well, maybe thor no better than us son, but thor not on casual. They've got positions. Davy it's yor place on the bus. Don't end up like yor da.

DAVY: Nowt wrong wi' me da.

MA: Nowt wrong wi' donkeys, but the' divven let them on busses.

DAVY: Sooner hev me da, than any o' them in the Toon Clerk's. All paper hankies for snot rags.

MA: Davy! Divven be si coarse.

DAVY: Ma, hev ye seen them? Stuck in thor desks. No proper winders ti look out. All that frosty glass, like the' hev in bogs. Pathetic! Sittin' pretendin' ti be doin' summick important. All the time, starin' sideways, ti see who's comin', an' gannin', wishin' it was thorselves. Might as well be at skule.

MA: School, Davy. School, not skule.

DAVY: All right! School, skule, what's the difference?

MA: A'll tell ye what the difference is. It's when the' go home at night. Thor not comin' ti the Ridges estate. No, they're livin' where flowers has the chance o' growin', an' a young laddie like you isn't just summick the polis has ti keep an eye on. Where ye can hev respect, an' yor own front door, an nee female welfare supervisor demandin' ti be in, ti cut yor pride off at the knees. Aye, by God, that's the dif'rence. (*Pause. She moves across to the window to glance out*) Aye, an' when the' hang thor washin' oot in the mornin', it's still there at dinner time.

DAVY: Ma, yor a patter merchant. Should hev ye on the tele.

MA: Ridges estate! What are wi? Just a joke. Ridges estate! Them that keeps thor coals in the bath. Go to a store for credit. Ridges estate? The' don't want ti know. Go for a decent job. Ridges estate? No chance.

DAVY: How come A got that interview then?

MA: That proves yor somethin' special, Davy. Somebody seen ye were dif'rent. Somebody's took a fancy ti ye.

DAVY: Hold on, ma. Don't want nobody fancyin' us.

MA: Son, it's your chance in life. Ye don't want a dead end job. Toss away all your education. All that study. Don't let yourself down Davy, an' don't let me down.

DAVY: Ma, yor not on. Things isn't like that now.

MA: Like what?

DAVY: Gettin' a good job in an office. Security, all that jazz. That went out wi' trams. Thor's better money on the docks.

MA: Aye, an' how long will that last? Thor clawin' each other's back now, for a share o' the meat.

DAVY: A can get twenty pound a week startin' money on the quay.

MA: Little apples, Davy. That's yor da talkin', an' it's little apples.

DAVY: An' extras.

MA: What extras?

DAVY: A bit fiddle.

MA (*Outraged*): Fiddle! What's a laddie like you talkin' about fiddle?

DAVY: Nowt wrong wi' fiddle. Not like pinchin', it's just… fiddle. Da says every job on the quay has ti have a fiddle, or the' cannot keep the men.

MA: Well, it sounds more like Mantovani's bloody orchestra ti me.

DAVY: Aw, ma!

MA: Now look, A'm havin' no argument. You were brought up ti touch nothin' that doesn't belong ye. Yor keepin' away from it. The fish quay is nowt but the home o' the forty thieves, an' A nivvor brought ye into the world ti be a fiddler.

Offstage, DA *can be heard returning. He is a robust, friendly man, only aggressive when frustrated. Heavy with drink, he is singing. His pocket bulges with a bottle of brown ale and with his filleting knife wrapped in a cloth. The sleeves of his jacket are sawn off at the elbows, in the manner of all fish filleters, to keep them from dipping into the trough.*

DA (*Offstage*): 'It's not unusual ti be loved by anyone, da, dee dee da.'

MA: Gawd! an' here comes the forst violin.

DA: 'Not unusual, ti be loved by anyone, an' if ye….'

The door opens and DA *enters. He resonantly belches.*

MA: That's lovely! Lovely A must say. Gi yor family the benefit o' yor company.

DA (*Smiling with the satisfaction of the belch*): That's me. That's yor da. Why give it away ti strangers. (*He advances on* MA. *Takes hold of her in a clumsy embrace. Forces her to dance. Sings*) 'Strangers in the night, da, da, dee dee da, strangers in the night'.

MA (*Forcing herself free*): Gerroff ye great puddin'. (*She goes off into the kitchen.* DA *takes off his jacket, puts it round the back of his chair and plants his bottle of brown ale on the table.*)

DA: Puttin' that kettle on or what?

MA (*Offstage*): A'm puttin' the kettle on.

DA: Worra woman. Hellow Davy! That's my bonny lad. (*Ruffles his son's hair*) All right, son?

DAVY: All right, da.

DA: That's my Davy. All right, son. Yor a good'n. Hey, no kiddin', ye did yor da proud this mornin'. (MA *comes in to catch the comment*) Oooo' sorry. (*Absurd gesture of secrecy*) Nuff sed!

DAVY: S' all right, da. She knows A was on the quay.

MA: Yor encouragin' him to go down there.

DA: Me?

MA: Yes, you

DA: Not me.

MA: Fine example you are.

DA: Ma, A've telled ye. That laddie's got his own mind ti make up. He'll do what he wants ti do, and gan where he wants ti gan.

MA: He's goin' for that interview.

DA: What interview?

MA: Ye know fine well what interview. The Town Clerk's.

DA: The (*Scornfully*) Toon Clerk's.

MA: Yes, the Toon Clerk's an' he's goin' for that interview.

DA: Ye've sayed that already.

She goes back into the kitchen making a decisive clatter of crockery.

DA (*Calling after her*): Ma, wor Davy's a sunshine lad. Y'know. 'E likes it oot in the fresh air, where the seagulls is flying roond. Huh', thor's no bloody seagulls in the toon clerk's.

MA (*Offstage*): 'Course thor's not, ye dope. What would the' be wantin' wi seagulls. Dirty, shitty things.

DA (*Taken aback by the vehemence*): That grub comin', or what.

MA (*Offstage*): A've telled ye it's comin'.

DA: So's Chris'mas.

MA: Alice come here, give's a hand.

ALICE *goes through to the kitchen to help bring in the plates of food.*

DA (*To* DAVY): Tell ye what. She'll have you in a bowler hat, wi' stripey pants.

DAVY: Not me.

DA: Gi' yor mates a laugh.

DAVY: Not likely.

DA: Toon Clerk's! Call that work? Ye bugs! Sittin' on thor backsides all day, pushin' a pen. Work! Hey! see what me an big Mutt lifted on the Grimsby wagon, eh? Ten ton! Ten bloody ton! Box, by box. None o' yor fancy fork lifts. Hundredweight, by hundredweight. Aye, an' the rain beatin' on wi. Now, that's what ye call work. Not a writer born, can write that down.

MA (*Offstage*): What ye sayin' to him?

DA (*Calling back*): Trouble we' you, ma, ye place too much store on education. Yor tryin' ti be upstairs, an' doonstairs at the same time. An' what di ye get? Stuck on the landin'.

62

DAVY and DA enjoy the joke. MA comes in with the food and they all gather at the table. MA plants DA's plateful savagely in front of him.

MA: Just fill yor gob wi' chips, an' let's have the biggest relief since Dunkirk. That bairn's goin' ti make use o' his education.

DA: Education!

MA: Alice! Davy! Sit down, get yor grub.

DA: A'll tell ye somethin' about education. (*He speaks between mouthfuls of food*) It's no good ti the workin' class. Thor's two kinds of education. The kind the give ti us, and the kind the keep for thorselves. An' the kind the give ti us, yor better off withoot.

MA: What do you know about education?

DA: Don't talk ti me about education.

MA: What would be the point?

DA: Listen, what di ye think the idea is? So's we can better worselves? Don't kid on. Listen, the idea of education, is ti make the likes of us, useful ti the buggars that's gettin' the money. Education! Education don't make the job fit you. Education makes you fit the job. Listen, them desks in the Toon Clerk's was there long before he was born. Education! Puts ye at a desk, or on a machine, an' that's what's wrong wi' this country. Too many machines, an' too many in bloody offices. (*DA reaches round for his jacket. He removes his filleting knife from the pocket and unrolls the cloth covering it*)

DA: Look, A'll show ye. There ye are. That's all ye need, a good filleting knife. That's the instrument. Carve yorsel' a career.

MA: What di ye want, bringing a wicked thing like that here.

DA: That's how ye cut 'em. (*He demonstrates the filleting of a fish*)

MA: Put it down.

DA: Poetry in motion. All hand cut, an' nothin' but the best.

MA: Put it away.

DA: A mean it's a simple thing a knife. Eh? But what was ever invented that's more effective.

*   *   *

Later.

DAVY: Da! A've gotta job! A've gotta job, da.

DA looks at DAVY uncomprehendingly.

63

DA: What you talkin' about. Job! What job!

DAVY: A've gotta job, da. Bob Wilson set us on.

DA: Eh?

DAVY: Gotta job on the quay wi' Bob Wilson.

MA: Davy, what ye sayin'?

DAVY: A'm sorry, ma.

MA: Davy!

DA: What ye talkin' about, Bob sayed nothin' ti me.

DAVY: Right enough, da. After ye'd gone 'e asked us if A wanted a start.

MA: Ye see. Ye see what ye've done.

DA: A've told ye, woman, A know nothin' about it. (*To* DAVY) Look, A'm yor father. Now A'm entitled ti know what's goin' on.

DAVY: He's startin' four school leavers on Monday. He's got three. He asked us if A wanted the job. Twenty pounds a week.

DA: Oh, Davy, what ye done?

DAVY: Twenty pounds, ma. It's ownly twelve at the Town Clerk's. It's another eight quid. (*Pause*)

DA: Well, A know nothin' about it. Nothin'. (*Pause*) Anyhow, what's Bob wantin' wi four young laddies?

DAVY: He's puttin' a machine in.

DA: Machine? What machine?

DAVY: A filletin' machine, da.

There is a pause as DA *struggles with the news.*

DA: A what?

DAVY: A filletin' machine, da. Bob says ye just feed the fish in, it goes thro' the machine, an' comes out the other end all cut.

DA: A know what a filletin' machine is.

DAVY: There's no experience necessary.

Pause.

DA: Ye bugs. Nobody tells ye nothin' ti yor face.

DAVY: Bob says thor installin' it this week-end. 'E reckons it'll cut fifty stone an hour.

Pause.

DA: Why is it? Nobody tells ye nothin' ti yor face.

DAVY: Reckons it's fantastic. Even small fish. Just rattles them thro'.

64

DA: S'what gets me. The' cannot come out with it.

DAVY: Has these nylon gears.

DA: Fifty stone an hour eh?

DAVY: That's what Bob says.

DA: Aye, well that's more'n a filleter's day's work.

DAVY: Bob says the blades are....

DA: Oh, ti hell wi' what Bob says.

   Pause.

MA: Davy! Get away out.

DAVY: What's the matter, ma.

MA: Go on, get away out.

DAVY: What've A done? A mean....

MA: Just get away out, Davy. Don't bother your Da.

DAVY (*Disgruntled*): A dunno! What we' always fightin' for? (*He leaves and* DA *slumps in a chair*)

DA: Nivvor ti yor face, that's what gets me. If they'd just come an' tell ye ti yor face.

   MA *resumes her tidying up.*

MA: Some things the' cannot say to a man's face.

DA: There was talk, like – ye know. Thor's always talk. But nobody ever comes out straight with it.

MA: A'll pour ye out a fresh cup o' tea.

DA: No. Don't bother.

MA: It's no bother. Look, it's still hot.

DA: No. It's all right. Look.... (*Awkward pause*) I'm sorry about the mess.

MA: It's all right. Big seas rock the little boats. (*She pours him out a fresh cup of tea. He is hunched over and she has to go close to him to offer the tea. This is a moment of truth. Despite the abusive row, when the chips are down,* MA *is the support figure*) Here!

DA: Ta! (*He takes the tea with one hand. With his other hand he reaches her.... He does not drink his tea but nurses it in his hands. The door opens and* ALICE *enters*)

MA: Told you ti stay out an' mind the bairn.

ALICE: Met Danny Mac. Sent us up with a message for da.

DA: Message? What message?

ALICE: 'E says, 'Tell yor da from Bob Wilson, not ti bother comin' down on Monday, 'cos thor's nowt expected'.

Pause. DA *looks pathetically at* MA. *He is shattered.*

DA: Ye buggar! Eh! Danny Mac! What's the matter wi' them? Bob tells Danny Mac. Danny Mac he tells her. What's the matter, the' cannot come and tell me ti me face?

MA: Mevves be a bit hard ti tell a man to his face ... (*Regretting what she is committed to say*) that he's not wanted.

Tom Hadaway

17

The Ugly Child

I heard them say I'm ugly.
I hoped it wasn't true.
I looked into the mirror
To get a better view,
And certainly my face seemed
Uninteresting and sad.
I *wish* that either it was good
Or else just very bad.

My eyes are green, my hair is straight,
My ears stick out, my nose
Has freckles on it all the year,
I'm skinny as a hose.
If only I could look as I
Imagine I might be.
Oh, all the crowds would turn and bow,
They don't – because I'm me.

Elizabeth Jennings

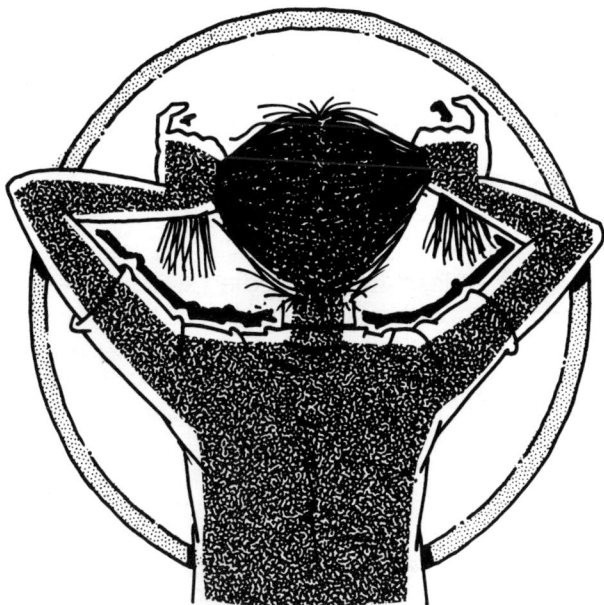

18
Tug-of-War

The following Saturday morning Arif stood in front of the full-length mirror in his bedroom, admiring his reflection. He felt his room didn't show him off to advantage. It looked shabby and reflected the taste of an earlier Arif when vintage cars on the wallpaper had been the height of his ambition. Recently, he'd seen some wallpaper that looked like leopard skin. He'd like it everywhere – over the walls, over the ceiling, even over the door so that you wouldn't be able to see easily how to get out. He'd read somewhere that that was useful when you brought girls to your room. Girls to your room! Huh! Fat chance of that with his mother's eagle eye on him. Besides, it had to be faced, he didn't know any girls who'd agree to come anywhere near his house, never mind his room.

He looked critically at himself now. Yes, there was no doubt about it, he was quite flash. Perhaps he'd be the first Asian rock star. Then he'd have real leopard skin everywhere, so that the door handle would be lost in the fur! He was wearing black trousers with a broad waistband, very tight on his hips. With this he wore a white grandpa shirt fastened casually at the neck with a button-badge. Arif muttered to himself as he remembered how stupid his mother had been at breakfast. Sometimes he wondered if she said things on purpose just to make him look small. 'Oh, Arif,' she'd said, 'wait before you go out. I'll sew a button on that shirt for you. You should've told me that you'd lost one. You can see there's a button missing. It looks really scruffy.'

Thoughtfully, Arif tied a red and brown scarf round his neck. No, hopeless, it hid his badge. His mind went back to the breakfast table. At least he'd wheedled some money out of his mother to go to Dope, his favourite shop in town. He supposed she was useful for some things. Mind you, he was pretty sure that he had his father to thank for that. His dad was softer than his mum. He'd heard him telling his mum not to go on at Arif so. 'He's growing up, Leila,' his father had said. 'We'll have to be careful.'

Yes, thought Arif grimly, his mother would have to be very careful. What a time he'd had with her, even when he was small, even when he was only seven and they had just come to this country. She'd always crossed him in what he wanted. Like the bike, he thought bitterly. He still felt angry about the bike.

He remembered the day they flew into London as clearly as if it had been yesterday. Life had become just too expensive in Kenya. The private school where his brother went had put up their fees again. His parents couldn't afford for Arif to go too.

'It's no good,' he could remember his father saying. 'We'll have to go to England. The boys will get a good education there and we won't have to pay anything for it.'

Arif's uncle was already in London. In no time at all, it had seemed to Arif, his mother, his brother and he were on the plane, leaving behind his father who would join them later. Really, that was when the trouble with his mother had started, thought Arif. He had not enjoyed it at all when she had suddenly become the one who told him what he could and could not do. When he was rude, she was furious – far crosser than his father had ever been with him.

The first incident in the tussle had been that of the bike. Arif was fantastically excited when at last they had left the airport. His uncle drove them round the back streets to his home and early on Arif had seen this lad no older than he, riding a bike such as he had never seen before – shiny, low, expensive-looking. It had symbolised Britain in a moment to Arif, and since then it seemed as if he had done nothing but want things and his mother has done nothing but try to thwart his wishes. At the time he had said out loud, 'I'm having one of those.'

'We've got to find somewhere to live first,' his mother said grimly.

It was like a slap in the face. Somewhere to live? That was ridiculous. They'd had quite a big house in Kenya. They were quite well off, really. Why was his mother talking such rubbish? Just to stop him having a bike, he knew.

But then they didn't find anywhere to live. His mother kept going to look at flats. When she rang up about them it seemed all right but as soon as she went to see the landlords, the arrangement fell through. 'Have you any children?' was always the question that cropped up – and then, 'We don't let to women with children. Sorry.'

It was all very mysterious. And somehow Arif was sure it was his mother's fault. He missed his dad. His missed his mates. And he wanted a bike.

At last, to cheer up his mother, his auntie had said, 'Next time you go for a flat say you've got two cats. They might not like that but at least if they agree to have you they might assume you haven't any children.'

Arif's mother thought she'd have a go. She made an appointment to see a flat. Straightaway when she met the landlord she said, 'I have to tell you I'm afraid I have two cats.'

'That's all right, Missis.' He was quite a nice gentleman for a change. 'Good of you to mention it. There's plenty as don't!'

And it had worked. He had quite forgotten to ask about children. How his mother and aunt had laughed about it! And for two months the landlord hadn't even known she had children!

Arif was surprised to find himself smiling as he remembered that, and feeling quite warm towards his mother. He must be getting soft. Well, and why not? She was a clever little thing, really. And brave. And pretty. She wasn't so bad, he supposed.

His dad had joined them after six months. Those had been great days. In particular he had liked Friday nights when his father and brother had taken him to the mosque. It had been fun travelling on the tube.

He didn't like going to the mosque nowadays. Somehow he couldn't learn his Koran and he often wriggled out of going. It was so shaming – even the seven-year-old boys knew more than he did. His father didn't insist, but Arif knew he was sorry. There were some very pretty girls at the mosque, though. He would say that for it. But there had been complaints about them, he knew, because he'd overheard his parents talking. He had a feeling that they were part of the reason his father didn't insist on his going. Pity, really, that he didn't see more of them. They were friendly girls. You didn't meet many girls like that who were pretty and smart too.

He thought of the Asian girl he was going to marry. She only existed in his mind as yet. But she'd be terrific. He'd be a famous dress designer and she would be his model.

Where would he meet her? In London? They'd moved away from there to Leicester when his father had arrived and they could afford to start buying their own house. London was best, though. The shops. The discos. The lights of Piccadilly. Would he meet her in Africa? Would he ever go back? Not for the first time Arif felt glad that he had come to England. He knew his life in Africa would have been entirely different. No discos, no flash gear, no rock. With an insight unusual for him, Arif realised that if he'd been in Africa now he'd still have been just a little boy. How pleased my mum would have been, he thought grimly.

Pop music! It was his life nowadays. He looked lovingly at his Throttlers' poster on the wall. Magic! He flicked a comb through his hair. He smiled his knock-out smile. God, the girls didn't stand a chance!

Susan Gregory and Jill Tilling

19

The Member of the Wedding

She stood before the mirror and she was afraid. It was the summer of fear, for Frankie, and there was one fear that could be figured in arithmetic with paper and a pencil at the table. This August she was twelve and five-sixths years old. She was five feet five and three-quarter inches tall, and she wore a number seven shoe. In the past year she had grown four inches, or at least that was what she judged. Already the hateful little summer children hollered to her: 'Is it cold up there?' And the comments of grown people made Frankie shrivel on her heels. If she reached her height on her eighteenth birthday, she had five and one-sixth growing years ahead of her. Therefore, according to mathematics and unless she could somehow stop herself, she would grow to be over nine feet tall. And what would be a lady who is over nine feet high? She would be a Freak.

*   *   *

'Do you think I will grow into a Freak?' Frankie whispered.

'You?' said Berenice again. 'Why, certainly not, I trust Jesus.'

Frankie felt better. She looked sidewise at herself in the mirror. The clock ticked six slow times, and then she said: 'Well, do you think I will be pretty?'

'Maybe. If you file down them horns a inch or two.'

Frankie stood with her weight resting on her left leg, and she slowly shuffled the ball of her right foot on the floor. She felt a splinter go beneath the skin. 'Seriously,' she said.

'I think when you fill out you will do very well. If you behave.'

'But by Sunday,' Frankie said. 'I want to do something to improve myself before the wedding.'

'Get clean for a change. Scrub your elbows and fix yourself nice. You will do very well.'

Frankie looked for a last time at herself in the mirror, and then she turned away. She thought about her brother and the bride, and there was a tightness in her that would not break.

'I don't know what to do. I just wish I would die.'

'Well, die then!' said Berenice.

And: 'Die', John Henry echoed in a whisper.

The world stopped.

'Go home,' said Frankie to John Henry.

He stood with his big knees locked, his dirty little hand on the edge of the white table, and he did not move.

'You heard me,' Frankie said. She made a terrible face at him and grabbed the frying pan that hung above the stove. She chased him three times around the table, then up through the front hall and out of the door. She locked the front door and called again: 'Go home.'

'Now what makes you act like that?' asked Berenice. 'You are too mean to live.'

Frankie opened the door to the stairway that led up to her room, and sat down on one of the lower steps. The kitchen was silent and crazy and sad.

'I know it,' she said. 'I intend to sit still by myself and think over everything for a while.'

Carson McCullers

73

20

Flight

One day off-handedly her sister told her
she was fat. Sixteen years old,
construing her adolescence in the mirror
and deciding she objected to the mould
and curve of breast and thigh,
she took to muesli, oranges and lettuce,
lost thirty pounds in sixty days,
tucking in jeans instead of food. 'Don't fuss,'
she told her mother, who called it 'Just a phase.'
Father, table-thumping, predicted she would die.

Thin as a sparrow, secretive as a water-rail,
with pointed nose and elongated toes,
she pecked her food, grew pale,
sprouted fingered wings and rose
one day from family noise and bother
to flutter through the open kitchen window,
circling and soaring high into the sky.
Father, preoccupied, failed to see her go.
Mother remarked, 'I'm not surprised. Our Di
ate just like a bird.' 'How absurd!' said father.

Mother it was who missed her most, pattering
round the house beslippered every evening,
leaving the cage-door open and scattering
bird-seed on a plate. But too little and too late.

Ken Morrice

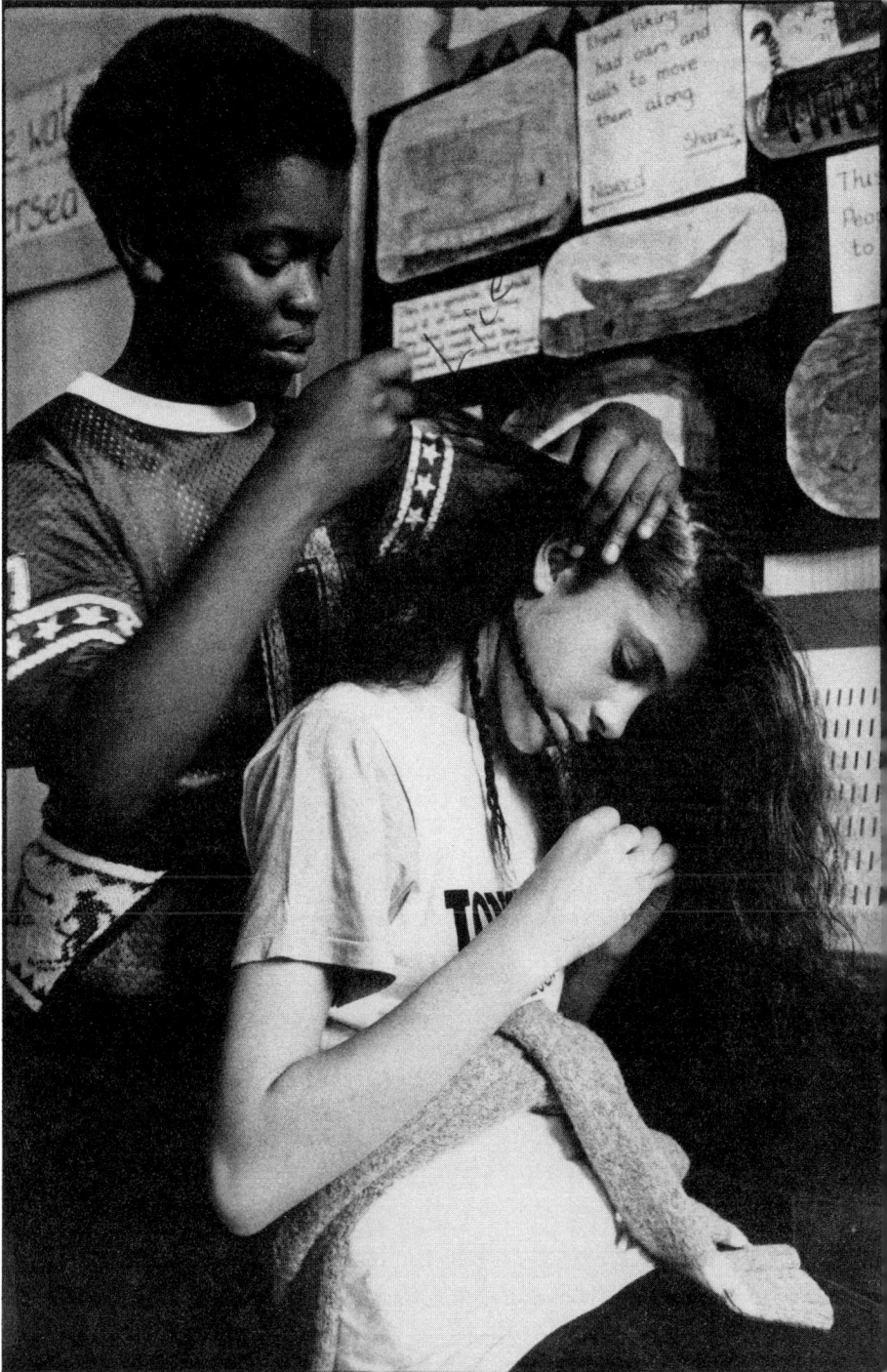

First Ice

A girl freezes in a telephone booth.
In her draughty overcoat she hides
A face all smeared
In tears and lipstick.

She breathes on her thin palms.
Her fingers are icy. She wears earrings.

She'll have to go home alone, alone,
Along the icy street.

First ice. It is the first time.
The first ice of telephone phrases.

Frozen tears glitter on her cheeks –
The first ice of human hurt.

Andrey Voznesensky

Lady of Shalott

Fifteen or younger
she moons in the mirror.
Penny for your thoughts,
Lady of Shalott.
In her bedroom tower
with mother and father
watching TV downstairs,
she moons in the mirror
and swears she will never
lead a bloody boring life like theirs.

Maybe you'll find True Romance
at the youth club dance,
Lady of Shalott.

She paints her nails scarlet,
she moons in the mirror.
Ingenue or harlot?
The mirror is misted,
every mirror image twisted.
Like Real Life – but larger.
That kid-glove
dream love
a Knight on a Charger.
Sure
you can lure
him, keep him enslaved.
Buy him Christmas aftershave.

She moons in the mirror
asks it to tell her
she's every bit as pretty as the other
gadfly girls.
Yes, you'll tangle him in your curls
my Lady of Shalott.

Maybe tonight's the night for
True Romance.
You'll find him at the youth club dance,
Lady of Shalott.

But alas
no handsome prince to dare
ask Rapunzel to let down her hair.
Her confidence cracked from side to side,
by twelve o'clock her tattered pride
is all Cinders stands in.
You're the wallflower the fellows all forgot,
Lady of Shalott.
Oh, how she wishes she could pass
like Alice through the looking glass.
You're waiting to be wanted,
my fairy-tale haunted
Lady of Shalott.

Silver dance shoes in her pocket,
no one's photo in her locket,
home alone through the night,
on either side suburban gardens lie,
bungalows and
bedded boxed-in couples high and dry.
But you're
lovely in the lamplight,
my Lady of Shalott.

Liz Lochhead

23

Charles

The day Laurie started kindergarten he renounced corduroy overalls with bibs and began wearing blue jeans with a belt; I watched him go off the first morning with the older girl next door, seeing clearly that an era of my life was ended, my sweet-voiced nursery-school tot replaced by a long-trousered, swaggering character who forgot to stop at the corner and wave goodbye to me.

He came home the same way, the front door slamming open, his cap on the floor, and the voice suddenly became raucous shouting, 'Isn't anybody *here*?'

At lunch he spoke insolently to his father, spilled Jannie's milk and remarked that his teacher said that we were not to take the name of the Lord in vain.

'How was school today?' I asked, elaborately casual.

'All right,' he said.

'Did you learn anything?' his father asked.

Laurie regarded his father coldly. 'I didn't learn nothing,' he said.

'Anything,' I said. 'Didn't learn anything.'

'The teacher spanked a boy, though,' Laurie said, addressing his bread and butter. 'For being fresh,'[1] he added with his mouth full.

'What did he do?' I asked. 'Who was it?'

Laurie thought. 'It was Charles,' he said. 'He was fresh. The teacher spanked him and made him stand in a corner. He was awfully fresh.'

'What did he do?' I asked again, but Laurie slid off his chair, took a cookie, and left, while his father was still saying, 'See here, young man.'

The next day Laurie remarked at lunch, as soon as he sat down, 'Well, Charles was bad again today.' He grinned enormously and said, 'Today Charles hit the teacher.'

'Good heavens,' I said, mindful of the Lord's name, 'I suppose he got spanked again?'

'He sure did,' Laurie said. 'Look up,' he said to his father.

---

[1] Impudent, cheeky.

'What?' his father said, looking up.

'Look down,' Laurie said. 'Look at my thumb. Gee, you're dumb.' He began to laugh insanely.

'Why did Charles hit the teacher?' I asked quickly.

'Because she tried to make him colour with red crayons,' Laurie said. 'Charles wanted to colour with green crayons so he hit the teacher and she spanked him and said nobody play with Charles but everybody did.'

The third day – it was Wednesday of the first week – Charles bounced a seesaw onto the head of a little girl and made her bleed and the teacher made him stay inside all during recess.[2] Thursday Charles had to stand in a corner during storytime because he kept pounding his feet on the floor. Friday Charles was deprived of blackboard privileges because he threw chalk.

On Saturday I remarked to my husband, 'Do you think kindergarten is too unsettling for Laurie? All this toughness and bad grammar, and this Charles boy sounds like such a bad influence.'

'It'll be all right,' my husband said reassuringly. 'Bound to be people like Charles in the world. Might as well meet them now as later.'

On Monday Laurie came home late, full of news. 'Charles,' he shouted as he came up the hill; I was waiting anxiously on the front steps; 'Charles,' Laurie yelled all the way up the hill, 'Charles was bad again.'

'Come right in,' I said, as soon as he came close enough. 'Lunch is waiting.'

'You know what Charles did?' he demanded, following me through the door. 'Charles yelled so in school they sent a boy in from first grade to tell the teacher she had to make Charles keep quiet, and so Charles had to stay after school. And so all the children stayed to watch him.'

'What did he do?' I asked.

'He just sat there,' Laurie said, climbing into his chair at the table. 'Hi Pop, y'old dust mop.'

'Charles had to stay after school today,' I told my husband. 'Everyone stayed with him.'

'What does this Charles look like?' my husband asked Laurie. 'What's his other name?'

'He's bigger than me,' Laurie said. 'And he doesn't have any

[2] Playtime.

rubbers and he doesn't ever wear a jacket.'

Monday night was the first Parent-Teachers meeting, and only the fact that Jannie had a cold kept me from going; I wanted passionately to meet Charles' mother. On Tuesday Laurie remarked suddenly, 'Our teacher had a friend come see her in school today.'

'Charles' mother?' my husband and I asked simultaneously.

'Naaah,' Laurie said scornfully. 'It was a man who came and made us do exercises. Look.' He climbed down from his chair and squatted down and touched his toes. 'Like this,' he said. He got solemnly back into his chair and said, picking up his fork, 'Charles didn't even *do* exercises.'

'That's fine,' I said heartily. 'Didn't Charles want to do exercises?'

'Naaah,' Laurie said. 'Charles was so fresh to the teacher's friend he wasn't *let* do exercises.'

'Fresh again?' I said.

'He kicked the teacher's friend,' Laurie said. 'The teacher's friend told Charles to touch his toes like I just did and Charles kicked him.'

'What are they going to do about Charles, do you suppose?' Laurie's father asked him.

Laurie shrugged elaborately. 'Throw him out of the school, I guess,' he said.

Wednesday and Thursday were routine; Charles yelled during story hour and hit a boy in the stomach and made him cry. On Friday Charles stayed after school again and so did all the other children.

With the third week of kindergarten Charles was an institution in our family; Jannie was being a Charles when she cried all afternoon; Laurie did a Charles when he filled his wagon full of mud and pulled it through the kitchen; even my husband, when he caught his elbow in the telephone cord and pulled telephone, ash tray, and a bowl of flowers off the table, said, after the first minute, 'Looks like Charles.'

During the third and fourth weeks there seemed to be a reformation in Charles; Laurie reported grimly at lunch on Thursday of the third week, 'Charles was so good today the teacher gave him an apple.'

'What?' I said, and my husband added warily, 'You mean Charles?'

'Charles,' Laurie said. 'He gave the crayons around and he picked up the books afterward and the teacher said he was her helper.'

'What happened?' I asked incredulously.

'He was her helper, that's all,' Laurie said, and shrugged.

'Can this be true, about Charles?' I asked my husband that night. 'Can something like this happen?'

'Wait and see,' my husband said cynically. 'When you've got a Charles to deal with, this may mean he's only plotting.'

He seemed to be wrong. For over a week Charles was the teacher's helper; each day he handed things out and he picked things up; no one had to stay after school.

'The PTA meeting's next week again,' I told my husband one evening. 'I'm going to find Charles' mother there.'

'Ask her what happened to Charles,' my husband said. 'I'd like to know.'

'I'd like to know myself,' I said.

On Friday of that week things were back to normal. 'You know what Charles did today?' Laurie demanded at the lunch table, in a voice slightly awed. 'He told a little girl to say a word and she said it and the teacher washed her mouth out with soap and Charles laughed.'

'What word?' his father asked unwisely, and Laurie said, 'I'll have to whisper it to you, it's so bad.' He got down off his chair and went around to his father. His father bent his head down

and Laurie whispered joyfully. His father's eyes widened.

'Did Charles tell the little girl to say *that*?' he asked respectfully.

'She said it *twice*,' Laurie said. 'Charles told her to say it *twice*.'

'What happened to Charles?' my husband asked.

'Nothing,' Laurie said. 'He was passing out the crayons.'

Monday morning Charles abandoned the little girl and said the evil word himself three or four times, getting his mouth washed out with soap each time. He also threw chalk.

My husband came to the door with me that evening as I set out for the PTA meeting. 'Invite her over for a cup of tea after the meeting,' he said. 'I want to get a look at her.'

'If only she's there,' I said prayerfully.

'She'll be there,' my husband said. 'I don't see how they could hold a PTA meeting without Charles' mother.'

At the meeting I sat restlessly, scanning each comfortable matronly face, trying to determine which one hid the secret of Charles. None of them looked to me haggard enough. No one stood up in the meeting and apologised for the way her son had been acting. No one mentioned Charles.

After the meeting I identified and sought out Laurie's kindergarten teacher. She had a plate with a cup of tea and a piece of chocolate cake; I had a plate with a cup of tea and a piece of marshmallow cake. We manoeuvred up to one another cautiously and smiled.

'I've been so anxious to meet you,' I said. 'I'm Laurie's mother.'

'We're all so interested in Laurie,' she said.

'Well, he certainly likes kindergarten,' I said. 'He talks about it all the time.'

'We had a little trouble adjusting, the first week or so,' she said primly, 'but now he's a fine little helper. With lapses, of course.'

'Laurie usually adjusts very quickly,' I said. 'I suppose this time it's Charles' influence.'

'Charles?'

'Yes,' I said laughing, 'you must have your hands full in that kindergarten, with Charles.'

'Charles?' she said. 'We don't have any Charles in the kindergarten.'

Shirley Jackson

83

24

Incident

Once riding in old Baltimore
Heart-filled, head-filled with glee,
I saw a Baltimorean
Keep looking straight at me.

Now I was eight and very small
And he was no whit bigger,
And so I smiled but he poked out
His tongue and called me, 'Nigger'.

I saw the whole of Baltimore
From May until December;
Of all the things that happened there
That's all that I remember.

Countee Cullen

25

After You, My Dear Alphonse

Mrs Wilson was just taking the gingerbread out of the oven when she heard Johnny outside talking to someone.

'Johnny,' she called, 'you're late. Come in and get your lunch.'

'Just a minute, Mother,' Johnny said. 'After you, my dear Alphonse.'

'After *you*, my dear Alphonse,' another voice said.

'No, after *you*, my dear Alphonse,' Johnny said.

Mrs Wilson opened the door. 'Johnny,' she said, 'you come in this minute and get your lunch. You can play after you've eaten.'

Johnny came in after her, slowly. 'Mother,' he said, 'I brought Boyd home for lunch with me.'

'Boyd?' Mrs Wilson thought for a moment. 'I don't believe I've met Boyd. Bring him in, dear, since you've invited him. Lunch is ready.'

'Boyd!' Johnny yelled. 'Hey, Boyd, come on in!'

'I'm coming. Just got to unload this stuff.'

'Well, hurry, or my mother'll be sore.'

'Johnny, that's not very polite to either your friend or your mother,' Mrs Wilson said. 'Come sit down, Boyd.'

As she turned to show Boyd where to sit, she saw he was a Negro boy, smaller than Johnny but about the same age. His arms were loaded with split kindling wood. 'Where'll I put this stuff, Johnny?' he asked.

Mrs Wilson turned to Johnny. 'Johnny,' she said, 'what did you make Boyd do? What is that wood?'

'Dead Japanese,' Johnny said mildly. 'We stand them in the ground and run over them with tanks.'

'How do you do, Mrs Wilson?' Boyd said.

'How do you do, Boyd? You shouldn't let Johnny make you carry all that wood. Sit down now and eat lunch, both of you.'

'Why shouldn't he carry the wood, Mother? It's his wood. We got it at his place.'

'Johnny,' Mrs Wilson said, 'go on and eat your lunch.'

'Sure,' Johnny said. He held out the dish of scrambled eggs to Boyd. 'After you, my dear Alphonse.'

'After *you*, my dear Alphonse,' Boyd said.

'After *you*, my dear Alphonse,' Johnny said. They began to giggle.

'Are you hungry, Boyd?' Mrs Wilson asked.

'Yes, Mrs Wilson.'

'Well, don't let Johnny stop you. He always fusses about eating, so you just see that you get a good lunch. There's plenty of food here for you to have all you want.'

'Thank you, Mrs Wilson.'

'Come on, Alphonse,' Johnny said. He pushed half the scrambled eggs on to Boyd's plate. Boyd watched while Mrs Wilson put a dish of stewed tomatoes beside his plate.

'Boyd don't eat tomatoes, do you, Boyd?' Johnny said.

'*Doesn't* eat tomatoes, Johnny. And just because you don't like them, don't say that about Boyd. Boyd will eat *anything*.'

'Bet he won't,' Johnny said, attacking his scrambled eggs.

'Boyd wants to grow up and be a big strong man so he can work hard,' Mrs Wilson said. 'I'll bet Boyd's father eats stewed tomatoes.'

'My father eats anything he wants to,' Boyd said.

'So does mine,' Johnny said. 'Sometimes he doesn't eat hardly anything. He's a little guy, though. Wouldn't hurt a flea.'

'Mine's a little guy, too,' Boyd said.

'I'll bet he's strong, though.' Mrs Wilson said. She hesitated. 'Does he ... work?'

'Sure,' Johnny said. 'Boyd's father works in a factory.'

'There, you see?' Mrs Wilson said. 'And he certainly has to be strong to do that – all that lifting and carrying at a factory.'

'Boyd's father doesn't have to,' Johnny said. 'He's a foreman.'

Mrs Wilson felt defeated. 'What does your mother do, Boyd?'

'My mother?' Boyd was surprised. 'She takes care of us kids.'

'Oh. She doesn't work, then?'

'Why should she?' Johnny said through a mouthful of eggs. 'You don't work.'

'You really don't want any stewed tomatoes, Boyd?'

'No, thank you, Mrs Wilson,' Boyd said.

'No, thank you, Mrs Wilson, no, thank you, Mrs Wilson, no thank you, Mrs Wilson,' Johnny said. 'Boyd's sister's going to work, though. She's going to be a teacher.'

'That's a very fine attitude for her to have, Boyd.' Mrs Wilson restrained an impulse to pat Boyd on the head. 'I imagine you're all very proud of her?'

'I guess so,' Boyd said.

'What about all your other brothers and sisters? I guess all of you want to make just as much of yourselves as you can.'

'There's only me and Jean,' Boyd said. 'I don't know yet what I want to be when I grow up.'

'We're going to be tank drivers, Boyd and me,' Johnny said. 'Zoom.' Mrs Wilson caught Boyd's glass of milk as Johnny's napkin ring, suddenly transformed into a tank, plowed heavily across the table.

'Look, Johnny,' Boyd said. 'Here's a foxhole. I'm shooting at you.'

Mrs Wilson, with the speed born of long experience, took the gingerbread off the shelf and placed it carefully between the tank and the foxhole.

'Now eat as much as you want to, Boyd,' she said. 'I want to see you get filled up.'

'Boyd eats a lot, but not as much as I do,' Johnny said. 'I'm bigger than he is.'

'You're not much bigger,' Boyd said. 'I can beat you running.'

Mrs Wilson took a deep breath. 'Boyd,' she said. Both boys turned to her. 'Boyd, Johnny has some suits that are a little too small for him, and a winter coat. It's not new, of course, but there's lots of wear in it still. And I have a few dresses that your mother or sister could probably use. Your mother can make them into lots of things for all of you, and I'd be very happy to give them to you. Suppose before you leave I make up a big bundle and then you and Johnny can take it over to your mother right away ...' Her voice trailed off as she saw Boyd's puzzled expression.

'But I have plenty of clothes, thank you,' he said. 'And I don't think my mother knows how to sew very well, and anyway I guess we buy about everything we need. Thank you very much, though.'

'We don't have time to carry that old stuff around, Mother,' Johnny said. 'We got to play tanks with the kids today.'

Mrs Wilson lifted the plate of gingerbread off the table as Boyd was about to take another piece. 'There are many little boys like you, Boyd, who would be very grateful for the clothes someone was kind enough to give them.'

'Boyd will take them if you want him to, Mother,' Johnny said.

'I didn't mean to make you mad, Mrs Wilson,' Boyd said.

'Don't think I'm angry, Boyd. I'm just disappointed in you, that's all. Now let's not say anything more about it.'

She began clearing the plates off the table, and Johnny took Boyd's hand and pulled him to the door. ''Bye, Mother,' Johnny said. Boyd stood for a minute, staring at Mrs Wilson's back.

'After you, my dear Alphonse,' Johnny said, holding the door open.

'Is your mother still mad?' Mrs Wilson heard Boyd ask in a low voice.

'I don't know,' Johnny said. 'She's screwy sometimes.'

'So's mine,' Boyd said. He hesitated. 'After *you*, my dear Alphonse.'

Shirley Jackson

26

Farmer's Boy

A doocot hung at the gable end of the byre. It had been untenanted for years, but a sudden whim of the Old Man to have pigeon pie on tap made it a source of pleasure and of a very characteristic type of altruism. By some means, fair or foul, but most likely foul, we raised enough capital to stock the cot with pigeons. They were delightful little persons as they strutted about the court picking up corn. I made a fantasy about them in which they were princesses charmed by a wicked fairy, and I have no doubt the Old Man made fantasies connected with pigeon pie. They were a grand investment, for they were not only beautiful but they also increased at a gratifying rate. The Old Man and I could never have done congratulating ourselves. We looked forward to the time when we would be the biggest pigeon owners in Scotland. We even thought there might be money in the business if we could train them to feed on our neighbours' corn. It was just then, when things were going so well, that my grandmother, with the touch of malice which even the best of women have, thought up a scheme for the good of our souls. Whenever any small boys came to visit Dungair, she would suggest that we give them a pair of doos to take home with them. The first time that happened the Old Man and I rose up in complete refusal. It was the most ridiculous idea that we had ever heard. But my grandmother insisted in her quiet way, the rest of the company agreed that it would be a pretty gesture and the small boy began to act as if the doos were his already. Some fool of a woman then said how nice it was to see such generosity in the young, and the pernicious small boy decided what pair he would have. The Old Man and I looked at each other in bitterness of heart. We had been manoeuvred into a false position. We could only accede to it as gracefully as we could. That brat of a child took our two best pigeons, but I am happy to say that I was able to push him into the midden before he left. The Old Man and I were in no very good humour when my grandmother told us we ought to be all of a glow because of our good deed. Dungair's reply was unprintable and I, though I had not the words, had much the same emotion. Yet the glow came when we least expected it, for the pigeons returned overnight.

'Aye, aye,' the Old Man said when I told him of the miracle, 'cast your bread upo' the waters...'

My grandmother never again had to suggest to us that we give away our pigeons to nasty little boys. We took an intense but secret delight in such generosity, and, if we gave away those doos once, we gave them away twenty times. They always came home by morning. It was a good game and a good moneymaker too, for some fathers were so pleased with my generosity that they tipped me a shilling, or even half-a-crown. Dungair made out a claim to a half-share of the tips, which I denied *in toto* and with heat, but I saw he had some justice on his side, so I bought him an ounce of Bogie Roll from the travelling grocer. That surprised him so much that he gave me a shilling, a thing he had never done before and never did again. Thus did I discover the value of a well-considered generosity.

J. R. Allan

27
The Potato Gatherers

November frost had starched the flat countryside into silent rigidity. The 'rat-tat-tat' of the tractor's exhaust drilled into the clean, hard air but did not penetrate it; each staccato sound broke off as if it had been nipped. Hunched over the driver's wheel sat Kelly, the owner, a rock of a man with a huge head and broken fingernails, and in the trailer behind were his four potato gatherers – two young men, permanent farm hands, and the two boys he had hired for the day. At six o'clock in the morning, they were the only living things in that part of County Tyrone.

The boys chatted incessantly. They stood at the front of the trailer, legs apart, hands in their pockets, their faces pressed forward into the icy rush of air, their senses edged for perception. Joe, the elder of the two – he was thirteen and had worked for Kelly on two previous occasions – might have been quieter, but his brother's excitement was infectious. For this was Philly's first job, his first time to take a day off from school to earn money,

his first opportunity to prove that he was a man at twelve years of age. His energy was a burden to him. Behind them, on the floor of the trailer, the two farm hands lay sprawled in half sleep.

Twice the boys had to cheer. The first time was when they were passing Dicey O'Donnell's house, and Philly, who was in the same class as Dicey, called across to the thatched, smokeless building, 'Remember me to all the boys, Dicey!' The second time was when they came to the school itself. It was then that Kelly turned to them and growled to them to shut up.

'Do you want the whole county to know you're taking the day off?' he said. 'Save your breath for your work.'

When Kelly faced back to the road ahead, Philly stuck his thumbs in his ears, put out his tongue, and wriggled his fingers at the back of Kelly's head. Then, suddenly forgetting him, he said, 'Tell me, Joe, what are you going to buy?'

'Buy?'

'With the money we get today. I know what I'm getting – a shotgun. Bang! Bang! Bang! Right there, mistah. Jist you put your two hands up above your head and I reckon you'll live a little longer.' He menaced Kelly's neck.

'Agh!' said Joe derisively.

'True as God, Joe. I can get it for seven shillings – an old one that's lying in Tom Tracy's father's barn. Tom told me he would sell it for seven shillings.'

'Who would sell it?'

'Tom.'

'Steal it, you mean. From his old fella.'

'His old fella has a new one. This one's not wanted.' He sighted along an imaginary barrel and picked out an unsuspecting sparrow in the hedge. 'Bang! Never knew what hit you, did you? What are you going to buy, Joe?'

'I don't know. There won't be much to buy with. Maybe – naw, I don't know. Depends on what Ma gives us back.'

'A bicycle, Joe. What about a bike? Quinn would give his away for a packet of cigarettes. You up on the saddle, Joe, and me on the crossbar. Out to the millrace every evening. Me shooting all the rabbits along the way. Bang! Bang! Bang! What about a bike, Joe?'

'I don't know. I don't know.'

'What did she give you back the last time?'

'I can't remember.'

'Ten shillings? More? What did you buy then? A leather belt? A set of rabbit snares?'

'I don't think I got anything back. Maybe a shilling. I don't remember.'

'A shilling! One lousy shilling out of fourteen! Do you know what I'm going to buy?' He hunched his shoulders and lowered his head between them. One eye closed in a huge wink. 'Tell no one? Promise?'

'What?'

'A gaff. See?'

'What about the gun?'

'It can wait until next year. But a gaff, Joe. See? Old Philly down there beside the Black Pool. A big salmon. A beaut. Flat on my belly, and – *phwist!* – there he is on the bank, the gaff stuck in his guts.' He clasped his middle and writhed in agony, imitating the fish. Then his act switched suddenly back to cowboys and he drew from both holsters at a cat sneaking home along the hedge. 'Bang! Bang! That sure settled you, boy. Where *is* this potato territory, mistah? Ah want to show you hombrés what work is. What's a-keeping this old tractor-buggy?'

'We're jist about there, Mistah Philly, sir,' said Joe. 'Ah reckon you'll show us, OK. You'll show us.'

The field was a two-acre rectangle bordered by a low hedge. The ridges of potatoes stretched lengthwise in straight, black lines. Kelly unfastened the trailer and hooked up the mechanical digger. The two labourers stood with their hands in their pockets and scowled around them, cigarettes hanging from their lips.

'You two take the far side,' Kelly told them. 'And Joe, you and –' He could not remember the name. 'You and the lad there, you two take this side. You show him what to do, Joe.' He climbed up on the tractor seat. 'And remember,' he called over his shoulder, 'if the school-attendance officer appears, it's up to you to run. I never seen you. I never heard of you.'

The tractor moved forward into the first ridges, throwing up a spray of brown earth behind it as it went.

'Right,' said Joe. 'What we do is this, Philly. When the digger passes, we gather the spuds into these buckets and then carry the buckets to the sacks and fill them. Then back again to fill the buckets. And back to the sacks. OK, mistah?'

'OK, mistah. Child's play. What does he want four of us for? I could do the whole field myself – one hand tied behind my back.'

Joe smiled at him. 'Come on, then. Let's see you.'

'Just you watch,' said Philly. He grabbed a bucket and ran stumbling across the broken ground. His small frame bent over the clay and his thin arms worked madly. Before Joe had begun gathering, Philly's voice called to him. 'Joe! Look! Full already! Not bad, eh?'

'Take your time,' Joe called back.

'And look, Joe! Look!' Philly held his hands out for his brother's inspection. They were coated with earth. 'How's that, Joe? They'll soon be as hard as Kelly's!'

Joe laughed. 'Take it easy, Philly. No rush.'

But Philly was already stooped again over his work, and when Joe was emptying his first bucket into the sack, Philly was emptying his third. He gave Joe the huge wink again and raced off.

Kelly turned at the bottom of the field and came back up. Philly was standing waiting for him.

'What you need is a double digger, Mr Kelly!' he called as the tractor passed. But Kelly's eyes never left the ridges in front of him. A flock of sea gulls swooped and dipped behind the tractor, fluttering down to catch worms in the newly turned earth. The boy raced off with his bucket.

'How's it going?' shouted Joe after another twenty minutes. Philly was too busy to answer.

A pale sun appeared about eight-thirty. It was not strong enough to soften the earth, but it loosened sounds – cars along the road, birds in the naked trees, cattle let out for the day. The clay became damp under it but did not thaw. The tractor exulted in its new freedom and its splutterings filled the countryside.

'I've been thinking,' said Philly when he met Joe at a sack. 'Do you know what I'm going to get, Joe? A scout knife with one of those leather scabbards. Four shillings in Byrne's shop. Great for skinning a rabbit.' He held his hands out from his sides now, because they were raw in places. 'Yeah. A scout knife with a leather scabbard.'

'A scout knife,' Joe repeated.

'You always have to carry a scout knife in case your gun won't fire or your powder gets wet. And when you're swimming underwater, you can always carry a knife between your teeth.'

'We'll have near twenty ridges done before noon,' said Joe.

'He should have a double digger. I told him that. Too slow, mistah. Too doggone slow. Tell me, Joe, have you made up your mind yet?'

'What about?'

'What you're going to buy, stupid.'

'Aw, naw. Naw ... I don't know yet.'

Philly turned to his work again and was about to begin, when the school bell rang. He dropped his bucket and danced back to his brother. 'Listen! Joe! Listen!' He caught fistfuls of his hair and tugged his head from side to side. 'Listen! Listen! Ha, ha, ha! Ho, ho, ho! Come on, you fat, silly, silly scholars and get to your lessons! Come on, come on, come on, come on! No dallying! Speed it up! Get a move on! Hurry! Hurry! Hurry! "And where are the O'Boyle brothers today? Eh? Where are they? Gathering potatoes? What's that I hear? What? What?"'

'Look out, lad!' roared Kelly.

The tractor passed within inches of Philly's legs. He jumped out of its way in time, but a fountain of clay fell on his head and shoulders. Joe ran to his side.

'Are you all right, Philly? Are you OK?'

'Tried to get me, that's what he did, the dirty cattle thief. Tried to get me.'

'You OK, mistah? Reckon you'll live?'

'Sure, mistah. Take more'n that ole coyote to scare me. Come on, mistah. We'll show him what men we really are.' He shook his jacket and hair and hitched up his trousers. 'Would you swap now, Joe?'

'Swap what?'

'Swap places with those poor eejits back there?' He jerked his thumb in the direction of the school.

'No sir,' said Joe. 'Not me.'

'Nor me neither, mistah. Meet you in the saloon.' He swaggered off, holding his hands as if they were delicate things, not part of him.

They broke for lunch at noon. By then, the sun was high and brave but still of little use. With the engine of the tractor cut off, for a brief time there was a self-conscious silence, which became relaxed and natural when the sparrows, now audible, began to chirp. The sea gulls squabbled over the latest turned earth and a cautious puff of wind stirred the branches of the tall trees. Kelly adjusted the digger while he ate. On the far side of the field, the two labourers stretched themselves on sacks and conversed in monosyllables. Joe and Philly sat on upturned buckets. For lunch they each had half a scone of homemade soda bread, cut into thick slices and skimmed with butter. They washed it down with mouthfuls of cold tea from a bottle. After they had eaten, Joe threw the crusts to the gulls, gathered up the newspapers in which the bread had been wrapped, emptied out the remains of the tea, and put the bottle and the papers into his jacket pocket. Then he stood up and stretched himself.

'My back's getting stiff,' he said.

Philly sat with his elbows on his knees and studied the palms of his hands.

'Sore?' asked Joe.

'What?'

'Your hands. Are they hurting you?'

'They're OK,' said Philly. 'Tough as leather. But the clay's sore. Gets right into every cut and away up your nails.' He held his arms out. 'They're shaking,' he said. 'Look.'

'That's the way they go,' said Joe. 'But they'll – Listen! Do you hear?'

'Hear what?'

'Lunchtime at school. They must be playing football in the playground.'

The sounds of high, delighted squealing came intermittently when the wind sighed. They listened to it with their heads uplifted, their faces broadening with memory.

'We'll get a hammering tomorrow,' said Joe. 'Six on each hand.'

'It's going to be a scout knife,' Philly said. 'I've decided on that.'

'She mightn't give us anything back. Depends on how much she needs herself.'

'She said she would. She promised. Have you decided yet?'

'I'm still thinking,' said Joe.

The tractor roared suddenly, scattering every other sound.

'Come on, mistah,' said the older one. 'Four more hours to go. Saddle up your horse.'

'Coming. Coming,' Philly replied. His voice was sharp with irritation.

The sun was a failure. It held its position in the sky and flooded the countryside with light but could not warm it. Even before it had begun to slip to the west, the damp ground had become glossy again, and before the afternoon was spent, patches of white frost were appearing on higher ground. Now the boys were working automatically, their minds acquiescing in what their bodies did. They no longer straightened up; the world was their feet and the hard clay and the potatoes and their hands and the buckets and the sacks. Their ears told them where the tractor was, at the bottom of the field, turning, approaching. Their muscles had become adjusted to their stooped position, and as long as the boys kept within the estab-lished pattern of movement their arms and hands and legs and shoulders seemed to float as if they were free of gravity. But if something new was expected from the limbs – a piece of glass

to be thrown into the hedge, a quick stepping back to avoid the digger – then their bodies shuddered with pain and the tall trees reeled and the hedges rose to the sky.

Dicey O'Donnell gave them a shout from the road on his way home from school. 'Hi! Joe! Philly!'

They did not hear him. He waited until the tractor turned. 'Hi! Hi! Philly! Philly! Joe!'

'Hello,' Joe called back.

'Youse are for it the morrow. I'm telling youse. He knows where youse are. He says he's going to beat the scruff out of youse the morrow. Youse are in for it, all right. Blue murder! Bloody hell! True as God!'

'Get lost!' Joe called back.

'Aye, and he's going to report youse to the attendance officer, and your old fella'll be fined. Youse are ruined! Destroyed! Blue murder!'

'Will I put a bullet in him, mistah?' said Joe to Philly.

Philly did not answer. He thought he was going to fall, and his greatest fear was that he might fall in front of the tractor, because now the tractor's exhaust had only one sound, fixed forever in his head, and unless he saw the machine he could not tell whether it was near him or far away. The 'rat-tat-tat' was a finger tapping in his head, drumming at the back of his eyes.

'Vamoose, O'Donnell!' called Joe. 'You annoy us. Vamoose.'

O'Donnell said something more about the reception they could expect the next day, but he got tired of calling to two stooped backs and he went off home.

The last pair of ridges was turned when the sky had veiled itself for dusk. The two brothers and the two labourers worked on until they met in the middle. Now the field was all brown, all flat, except for the filled sacks that patterned it. Kelly was satisfied; his lips formed an O and he blew through them as if he were trying to whistle. He detached the digger and hooked up the trailer. 'All aboard!' he shouted, in an effort at levity.

On the way home, the labourers seemed to be fully awake, for the first time since morning. They stood in the trailer where the boys had stood at dawn, behind Kelly's head and facing the road before them. They chatted and guffawed and made plans for a dance that night. When they met people they knew along the way, they saluted extravagantly. At the crossroads, they began to wrestle, and Kelly had to tell them to watch out or they would fall over the side. But he did not sound angry.

Joe sat on the floor, his legs straight out before him, his back resting against the side of the trailer. Philly lay flat out, his head cushioned on his brother's lap. Above him, the sky spread out, grey, motionless, enigmatic. The warmth from Joe's body made him drowsy. He wished the journey home to go on forever, the sound of the tractor engine to anaesthetise his mind forever. He knew that if the movement and the sound were to cease, the pain of his body would be unbearable.

'We're nearly there,' said Joe quietly. 'Are you asleep?' Philly did not answer. 'Mistah! Are you asleep, mistah?'

'No.'

Darkness came quickly, and when the last trace of light disappeared the countryside became taut with frost. The head lamps of the tractor glowed yellow in the cold air.

'Philly? Are you awake, mistah?'

'What?'

'I've been thinking,' said Joe slowly. 'And do you know what I think? I think I've made up my mind now.'

One of the labourers burst into song.

'If I were a blackbird, I'd whistle and sing, and I'd follow the ship that my true love sails in.'

His mate joined him at the second line and their voices exploded in the stiff night.

'Do you know what I'm going to buy?' Joe said, speaking more loudly. 'If she gives us something back, that is. Mistah! Mistah Philly! Are you listening? I'm going to buy a pair of red silk socks.'

He waited for approval from Philly. When none came, he shook his brother's head. 'Do you hear, mistah? Red silk socks – the kind Jojo Teague wears. What about that, eh? What do you think?'

Philly stirred and half raised his head from his brother's lap. 'I think you're daft,' he said in an exhausted, sullen voice. 'Ma won't give us back enough to buy anything much. No more than a shilling. You knew it all the time.' He lay down again and in a moment he was fast asleep.

Joe held his brother's head against the motion of the trailer and repeated the words 'red silk socks' to himself again and again, nodding each time at the wisdom of his decision.

Brian Friel

28

Term Time

There's some that sing of the hiring fair
And sound out an alarm,
But the best old song that ever was sung
It is about the term.
The term time it is drawing near.
When we will all win free.
And with the hungry farmers
Again will never fee.

With broadtail coats and Quaker hats,
And whips below their arms,
They'll hawk and call the country round
A-seeking for their farms,
And they'll go on some twenty mile
Where people doesn't know 'em,
And there they'll hire their harvest hands,
And bring them far from home.

They'll tip you on the shoulder
And ask if you're to fee,
They'll tell you a fine story
That's every word a lie;
They'll tell you a fine story
And get you to perform
But, lads, when you are under them
It's like a raging storm.

On cabbage cold and taters
They'll feed you like the pigs
While they sit at their tea and toast,
And ride about in gigs.
The mistress must be 'Ma'am' and you
Must lift your cap to her;
And before you find an entrance
The master must get 'Sir'.

Traditional

29

The Breadwinner

The parents of a boy of fourteen were waiting for him to come home with his first week's wages.

The mother had laid the table and was cutting some slices of bread and butter for tea. She was a little woman with a pinched face and a spare body, dressed in a blue blouse and skirt, the front of the skirt covered with a starched white apron. She looked tired and frequently sighed heavily.

The father, sprawling inelegantly in an old armchair by the fireside, legs outstretched, was little too. He had watery blue eyes and a heavy brown moustache, which he sucked occasionally.

These people were plainly poor, for the room, though clean, was meanly furnished, and the thick pieces of bread and butter were the only food on the table.

As she prepared the meal, the woman from time to time looked contemptuously at her husband. He ignored her, raising his eyebrows, humming, or tapping his teeth now and then with his finger-nails, making a pretence of being profoundly bored.

'You'll keep your hands off the money,' said the woman, obviously repeating something that she had already said several times before. 'I know what'll happen to it if you get hold of it. He'll give it to me. It'll pay the rent and buy us a bit of food, and not go into the till at the nearest public-house.'

'You shut your mouth,' said the man, quietly.

'I'll not shut my mouth!' cried the woman, in a quick burst of anger. 'Why should I shut my mouth? You've been boss here for long enough. I put up with it when you were bringing money into the house, but I'll not put up with it now. You're nobody here. Understand? *Nobody. I'm* boss and he'll hand the money to me!'

'We'll see about that,' said the man, leisurely poking the fire.

Nothing more was said for about five minutes.

Then the boy came in. He did not look older than ten or eleven years. He looked absurd in long trousers. The whites of his eyes against his black face gave him a startled expression.

The father got to his feet.

'Where's the money?' he demanded.

The boy looked from one to the other. He was afraid of his father. He licked his pale lips.

'Come on now,' said the man. 'Where's the money?'

'Don't give it to him,' said the woman. 'Don't give it to him, Billy Give it to me.'

The father advanced on the boy, his teeth showing in a snarl under his big moustache.

'Where's that money?' he almost whispered.

The boy looked him straight in the eyes.

'I lost it,' he said.

'You – *what*?' cried his father.

'I lost it,' the boy repeated.

The man began to shout and wave his hands about.

'Lost it!*Lost it*! What are you talking about? How could you lose it?'

'It was in a packet,' said the boy, 'a little envelope. I lost it.'

'Where did you lose it?'

'I don't know. I must have dropped it in the street.'

'Did you go back and look for it?'

The boy nodded. 'I couldn't find it,' he said.

The man made a noise in his throat, half grunt, half moan – the sort of noise that an animal would make.

'So you lost it, did you?' he said. He stepped back a couple of paces and took off his belt – a wide, thick belt with a heavy brass buckle. 'Come here,' he said.

The boy, biting his lower lip so as to keep back the tears, advanced, and the man raised his arm. The woman, motionless until that moment, leapt forward and seized it. Her husband, finding strength in his blind rage, pushed her aside easily. He brought the belt down on the boy's back. He beat him unmercifully about the body and legs. The boy sank to the floor, but did not cry out.

When the man had spent himself, he put on the belt and pulled the boy to his feet.

'Now you'll get off to bed,' he said.

'The lad wants some food,' said the woman.

'He'll go to bed. Go and wash yourself.'

Without a word the boy went into the scullery and washed his hands and face. When he had done this he went straight upstairs.

The man sat down at the table, ate some bread and butter and drank two cups of tea. The woman ate nothing. She sat opposite him, never taking her eyes from his face, looking with hatred at him. Just as before, he took no notice of her, ignored her, behaved as if she were not there at all.

When he had finished the meal he went out.

Immediately he had shut the door the woman jumped to her feet and ran upstairs to the boy's room.

He was sobbing bitterly, his face buried in the pillow. She sat on the edge of the bed and put her arms about him, pressed him close to her breast, ran her fingers through his disordered hair, whispered endearments, consoling him. He let her do this, finding comfort in her caresses, relief in his own tears.

After a while his weeping ceased. He raised his head and smiled at her, his wet eyes bright. Then he put his hand under the pillow and withdraw a small dirty envelope.

'Here's the money,' he whispered.

She took the envelope and opened it and pulled out a long strip of paper with some figures on it – a ten shilling note and a sixpence.

Leslie Halward

My Friend Tom

My friend Tom's a bit of a laugh:
   There's a motorbike in his smile –
A rod that'll do a ton-and-a-half
   Over the Murder Mile.

My friend Tom's got an iron grip
   On the iron he rides through time:
When he runs people down his wheels hardly slip
   In the slosh of their mashed-up slime.

Cats that grin in the catseyed dark
   Die in a cushioned squeal,
While the dogs that chase them halve their bark.
   Sliced in two by the wheel.

My friend Tom's a skin for the girls
   They clench their knees on his seat
And burp up their beer on his sick leather gear
   While he blows like a gale down the street.

They like the tang of time on their face
   And the blood that shoots up their skirt.
Though some that have ridden behind him
   Lie ahead of him under the dirt.

Daff went straight at a corner,
   Dot carried on from a flips,
And on and then on through some railings
   In neat little vertical strips.

My friend Tom's a bit of a lad,
   And he's bit off a bit of his smile;
The rest of it's spread round the back of his head
   Which is spread round the Murder Mile.

Michael Baldwin

George and the Dragonfly

Georgie Jennings was spit almighty.
When the golly was good
he could down a dragonfly at 30 feet
and drown a 100 midges with the fallout.
At the drop of a cap
he would outspit lads
years older and twice his size.
Freckled and rather frail
he assumed the quiet dignity
beloved of schoolboy heroes.

But though a legend in his own playtime
Georgie Jennings failed miserably in the classroom
and left school at 15 to work for his father.
And talents such as spitting
are considered unbefitting
for upandcoming porkbutchers.

I haven't seen him since,
but like to imagine some summer soiree
when, after a day moistening mince,
George and his wife entertain tanned friends.
And after dinner, sherrytongued talk
drifts back to schooldays: the faces
halfrecalled, the adventures overexaggerated.

And the next thing,
that shy sharpshooter of days gone by
is led, vainly protesting, on to the lawn
where, in the hush of a golden august evening
a reputation, 20 years tall, is put to the test.
So he takes extra care as yesterheroes must,
fires, and a dragonfly, encapsulated, bites the dust.
Then amidst bravos and tinkled applause,
blushing, Georgie leads them back indoors.

Roger McGough

Executive

I am a young executive. No cuffs than mine are cleaner;
I have a Slimline brief-case and I use the firm's Cortina.
In every roadside hostelry from here to Burgess Hill
The *maîtres d'hôtel* all know me well and let me sign the bill.

You ask me what it is I do. Well actually, you know,
I'm partly a liaison man and partly P.R.O.
Essentially I integrate the current export drive
And basically I'm viable from ten o'clock till five.

For vital off-the-record work – that's talking transport-wise –
I've a scarlet Aston-Martin – and does she go? She flies!
Pedestrians and dogs and cats – we mark them down for
    slaughter.
I also own a speed-boat which has never touched the water.

She's built of fibre-glass, of course. I call her 'Mandy Jane'
After a bird I used to know – No soda, please, just plain –
And how did I acquire her? Well to tell you about that
And to put you in the picture I must wear my other hat.

I do some mild developing. The sort of place I need
Is a quiet country market town that's rather run to seed.
A luncheon and a drink or two, a little *savoir faire* –
I fix the Planning Officer, the Town Clerk and the Mayor.

And if some preservationist attempts to interfere
A 'dangerous structure' notice from the Borough Engineer
Will settle any buildings that are standing in our way –
The modern style, sir, with respect, has really come to stay.

John Betjeman

33

Telegraph Road

A long time ago came a man on a track
walking thirty miles with a sack on his back
and he put down his load where he thought it was the best
he made a home in the wilderness
he built a cabin and a winter store
and he ploughed up the ground by the cold lake shore
and the other travellers came riding down the track
and they never went further and they never went back
then came the churches then came the schools
then came the lawyers then came the rules
then came the trains and the trucks with their loads
and the dirty old track was the telegraph road

Then came the mines – then came the ore
then there was the hard times then there was a war
telegraph sang a song about the world outside
telegraph road got so deep and so wide
like a rolling river ...

And my radio says tonight it's gonna freeze
people driving home from the factories
there's six lanes of traffic
three lanes moving slow ...

I used to like to go to work but they shut it down
I've got a right to go to work but there's no work here to be found
yes and they say we're gonna have to pay what's owed
we're gonna have to reap from some seed that's been sowed
and the birds up on the wires and the telegraph poles
they can always fly away from this rain and this cold
you can hear them singing out their telegraph code
all the way down the telegraph road

You know I'd sooner forget but I remember those nights
when life was just a bet on a race between the lights
you had your head on my shoulder you had your hand in my hair
now you act a little colder like you don't seem to care ...
but believe in me baby and I'll take you away
from out of this darkness and into the day
from these rivers of headlights these rivers of rain

from the anger that lives on the streets with these names
'cos I've run every red light on memory lane
I've seen desperation explode into flames
and I don't wanna see it again ...

From all of these signs saying sorry but we're closed
all the way down the telegraph road

Mark Knopfler

Ofa Sunday

ofa sunday
the only thing
i burn
at both ends
is my bacon.
Like the tele
phone i am
off the hook

i watch the
newspapers for
hours & browse
through TV
miss mass
and wonder
if mass
misses me

Roger McGough

Vegetarians

Vegetarians are cruel, unthinking people.
Everybody knows that a carrot screams when grated.
That a peach bleeds when torn apart.
Do you believe an orange insensitive
to thumbs gouging its flesh?
That tomatoes spill their brains painlessly?
Potatoes, skinned alive and boiled,
the soil's little lobsters.
Don't tell me it doesn't hurt
when peas are ripped from the scrotum,
the hide flayed off sprouts,
cabbage shredded, onions beheaded.

Throw in the trowel
and lay down the hoe.
Mow no more
Let my people go!

Roger McGough

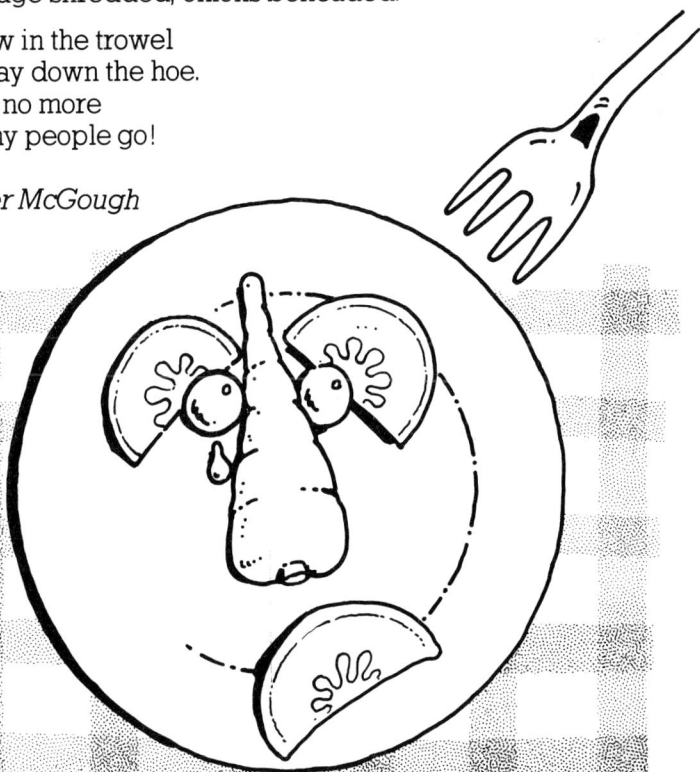

36

Something I'm Not

familiar with, the tune
of their talking, comes tumbling before them
down the stairs which (oh I forgot) it was my turn
to do again this week.
My neighbour and my neighbour's child. I nod, we're not
on speaking terms exactly.

I don't know much about her. Her dinners smell
different. Her husband's a busdriver,
so I believe.
She carries home her groceries in Grandfare bags
though I've seen her once or twice around the corner
at Shastri's for spices and such.
(I always shop there – he's open till all hours
making good). How does she feel?
Her children grow up with foreign accents,
swearing in fluent Glaswegian. Her face

is sullen. Her coat is drab plaid, hides
but for a hint at the hem, her sari's
gold embroidered gorgeousness. She has
a jewel in her nostril.
The golden hands with the almond nails
that push the pram turn blue
in this city's cold climate.

Liz Lochhead

37
Visiting

When we arrive she shows no surprise
Presents a cheek to be kissed
In tribute merely due
To an aged lady.

He goes to put the kettle on.

A silence, then
Head sharply to one side
She points an eye at me, pecking
At crumbs of scattered memories.

I have a sister, you know,
She tells me in triumph
Picking a random seed from the grain of years.
I know, of course – she is my mother
And this my aunt who does not recognise
The man who was the country nephew
Wide-eyed come to town
To see with her the latest Disney
And share banana sandwiches
Conspiratorially
In the flickering dark.

Once she made an oyster of her world
Trotted the globe on a cliché
Gathering no moss, she said,
A spinster rolling stone,
But gathered a man – this man
She does not recognise
Who brings the tea immaculately
Set on a silver tray, her sailor
Whose gold-ringed sleeve she clings to
Smiling for ever on the mantelpiece.

Now he stands an endless watch
Serving her eccentric whim
Patiently, caringly wiping the tea
Dribbled on her stained cardigan,
Making sure she is free from draughts
As her wandering mind sets sail
To voyage fitfully on errant winds.

Later, driving home, the radio plays
A Beatle asking
Will you still need me, will you still feed me
When I'm sixty-four?
And for a moment I do not understand
The look you gave me
Or the tears
That shone in your eyes.

Colin Lamont

Eighty-one Years Old

She wanted to die and all of us
Agree although we do not say;
Instead, we tend her every day,
Bring flowers and food without much fuss.
She stares at us and we stare back,
Each knowing what the others lack.

She cannot die. At times, her heart
Moves slowly, almost stops and then
The lingering life begins again,
New days of sickness have to start.
Someone must always be near by;
She must not be alone to die.

And that is what she longs for most –
To be alone, when no one stands
With filled but with unhelping hands.
Even the priest who brings the Host
Cannot provide the peace but stays
To join in mumbled words of praise.

An empty space, a dusted room –
These will be left when she at last
Becomes her own self-willed outcast.
And guilty thoughts, no doubt, will come
To nurses who had wished her dead
And now have nothingness instead.

Elizabeth Jennings

Man on a Bench

This old man
has grown year-weary
no joy in changing seasons, just
another blooming spring
another sodden summer
another corny old autumn
and another winter
to leave him cold.

Liz Lochhead

Home

in streets I once knew
the moon is trapped in an attic
and the net of stars is frozen
over an old house

an old man
rattles the fire's remains
in a shadowy room
smoking he draws his chair
to the black grate
sees streets he once knew
hears a child call his name

Paul Donnelly

Old Father

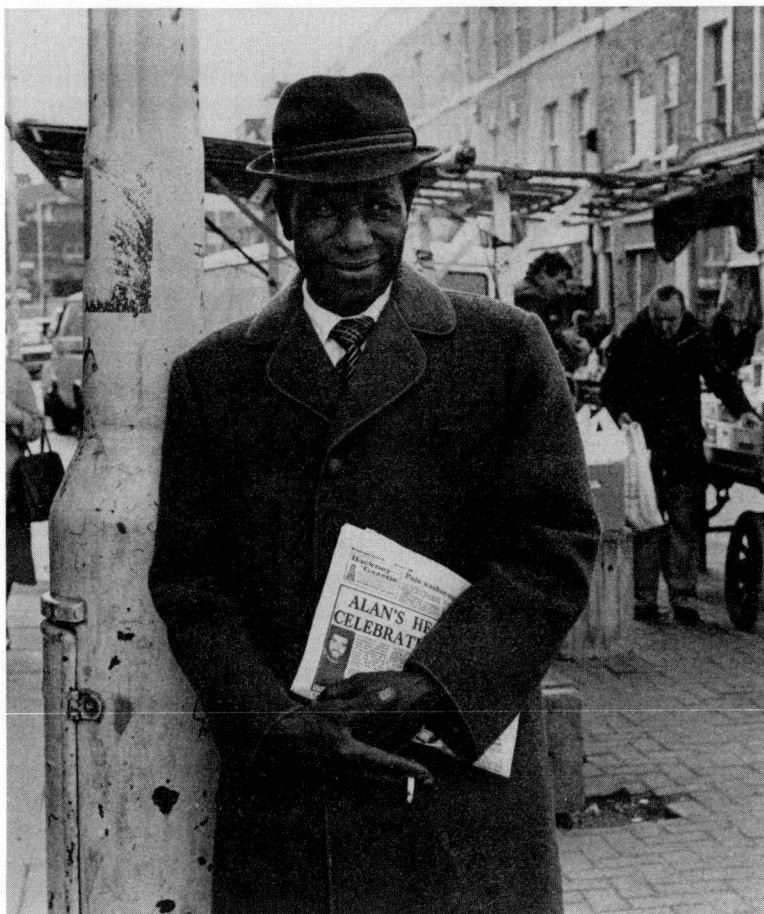

Old Father to England in Winter '59.
Cold bite him hard,
Make him bawl in his small basement room
By the Grove.
Every day he cry out:
'Man, a tekkin' de nex' boat back home.'
But come sping,
Old Father still here.

Time passed.
Old Father feet begin to shift.
His roots have no meaning now.
He straighten his hair,
Press it smooth.
Coloured girls no good for he –
Day after day you see him
Bouncing down the road with a blonde,
Never brunette,
And his suit, cream or beige,
Never anything dark.

Old Father don't mix with the boys
On Saturday night no more –
No, he sit in the pub up the road –
The one at the corner
That don't like serving black people –
And he crack joke with them white people on we.
'Tut tut,' he would say,
'Isn't it disgusting
How they make a spectacle of themselves
At cricket matches.'

He don't say 'Hello' no more,
Don't eat dasheen or yam –
'not very digestible' –
And Heaven forbid,
He even turn his back on
Saltfish with 'chove an' dumpling.

Boy,
Old Father don't want to know we now,
In his white Rover,
With his slicked-back hair.
And them white people saying
'He's an example to his people.'

Hugh Boatswain

Acknowledgements

The authors and publishers wish to thank the following for permission to reproduce copyright material. It has not been possible to contact all copyright holders, and the publishers would be glad to hear from any unacknowledged copyright holders.

John Farquharson Ltd for 'Grandmother' from *The Longships in Harbour* by William McIlvanney, published by Eyre and Spottiswoode; Polygon Books for Liz Lochhead's 'Poem for My Sister', 'The Choosing' and 'Something I'm Not' from *Dreaming Frankenstein* and *Collected Poems*; John Johnson Ltd for 'Lady of Shallot' and 'Man on a Bench' by Liz Lochhead; Century Hutchinson for the extracts from *A Child in the Forest* by Winifred Foley and *The Member of the Wedding* by Carson McCullers; Faber and Faber Publishers for 'My Papa's Waltz' by Theodore Roethke from *The Collected Poems of Theodore Roethke*; Murray Pollinger for the extract from *Danny, the Champion of the World* by Roald Dahl, published by Jonathan Cape and Puffin Books; Edward Storey for 'In Memory of My Grandfather'; the extract from *Luke Baldwin's Vow* by Morley Callaghan, and the poems 'George and the Dragonfly', 'Ofa Sunday' and 'Vegetarians' by Roger McGough are reprinted by permission of A. D. Peters & Co Ltd; A. M. Heath & Company Ltd for the extracts from *The Country Girls* by Edna O'Brien, published by Jonathan Cape, *Charles* and *After You, My Dear Alphonse* by the late Shirley Jackson and the poem 'My Friend Tom' by Michael Baldwin from *How Charles Egget Lost His Way in a Creation Myth*; the Scottish Examination Board for 'Pakistani'; Weidenfeld & Nicholson for the extract from *Clinging to the Wreckage* by John Mortimer; Hamish Hamilton Ltd for the extract from *How Many Miles to Babylon* by Jennifer Johnston; Andre Deutsch for the extract from *Comfort Herself* by Geraldine Kaye; Tom Hadaway for extracts from his play *The Filleting Machine*; David Higham Associates Ltd and Elizabeth Jennings for the poems 'Eighty One Years Old' from *Recoveries*, published by Macmillan, and 'The Ugly Child' from *The Secret Brother*, published by Carcanet Press and the short story *The Breadwinner* by Leslie Halward, published by Edward Arnold;

Illustrations